CrushThe Test

SAT Math Prep

Hard Questions For 700+

by Matthew Kohler Ph.D.

CrushTheTest · Boulder, Colorado

Cover Photograph: George Kourounis (www.stormchaser.ca)

Cover Design: Troup Wood

Cover Fire Pattern: Obsidian Dawn (www.obsidiandawn.com)

Cover Photoshop Work: Kari Rivers (Minuteman Press, Boulder)

First Web Publication: August 15, 2005

First Hardcopy Edition: April 2, 2007

ISBN: 1451574592

EAN-13: 9781451574593

About this Book

Any SAT* question is easy — once you see how to do it. The "hard" questions are not actually difficult but they *are* clever. Even if you are extremely proficient at math, a sufficiently clever question can send you down the wrong road and . . . ten minutes later you get the answer, but it's too late: the SAT "got" you.

Here's a classic example of a clever question that, once upon a time, "got" many a professional mathematician. It never appeared on an SAT but it does have that perfect blend of simple math and diabolical cleverness.

> Two trains are traveling towards each other at 60 mph. They are 1 mile apart. A fly sitting on the front of one train flies toward the other train at 120 mph. Upon reaching the second train, the fly instantly reverses direction and flies back to the first train. The fly flies back and forth between the trains until they collide. What is the total distance flown by the fly?**

Remember, <u>it has to be easy</u>.

The first CrushTheTest questions were created in 2001 for Dr. Matthew Kohler's SAT students who needed two things: 1) more "hard" questions and 2) many questions in a row of the same type. CrushTheTest questions are *all* hard and they come at you ten at a time in each category.

The CrushTheTest website went live in 2005; the first book was sold in 2007.

---

* SAT is a registered trademark of the College Board, which was not involved in the production of, and does not endorse, this product.

** A professional might be tricked into summing a series and would solve the problem in a few minutes. An SAT expert realizes that it takes 30 seconds for the trains to collide and, since the fly flies at 120 mph = 2 miles per minute, it travels 1 mile. A *super* SAT expert sees that the fly's speed is the same as the approach speed of the trains so the distances covered have to be the same!

About the Cover Photo

The cover photograph is the famous (and deadly) Komodo dragon. It was taken by intrepid explorer and photographer George Kourounis, who, for the sake of science and pleasure, risked his life to get close enough to this 10-foot-long lizard to snap the perfect photo.

Mr. Kourounis kindly granted CrushTheTest permission to use his photo.

George's website (www.stormchaser.ca) documents his travels chronicling Earth at its most extreme. It might be golf-ball sized hail, erupting volcanos, multiple tornados, or a 300-pound Komodo dragon with serrated teeth, toxic saliva, and an indiscriminate palate — George has gotten up close and personal.

Although no one has ever documented a wild Komodo devouring an SAT, we cannot say with certainty that such a thing has never happened. The hungry Komodo cover was designed by Troup Wood. A graduate of Peak to Peak High School in Boulder, Colorado and a former CrushTheTest student, Troup will join the Dartmouth class of 2014 this coming fall (2010).

The fire art on the cover was kindly provided by Obsidian Dawn which maintains a superb web site (www.obsidiandawn.com) with free tools for professional artists and enthusiastic amateurs.

According to the Smithsonian Institution (nationalzoo.si.edu), the Komodo's "basic strategy is simple: try to smash the quarry to the ground and tear it to pieces." We hope you'll do the same to the SAT.

Table of Contents: Book I

Why CrushTheTest?

You're cruising along on a 20-question math section on the real SAT. The first 17 questions weren't too bad. You are about to do questions 18, 19, and 20. This is IT: these are the hard questions. You know you have to get them right or kiss your 700+ goodbye. You dig in . . .

The Problem

Practice tests in *The Official SAT Study Guide*[1] have 8-10 hard questions. If you need a 700+, you don't get enough practice with the questions that will make or break your score. Also, official practice test questions are scattered by type. So you might see a vicious prime numbers question on one test and then not see a similar question until five tests later by which time the first vicious prime numbers question is a distant memory.

The Solution

CrushTheTest. Here are 210 hard SAT-style questions in twenty-one 10-question sections. Each section concentrates on one type of problem: vicious prime numbers questions, for example, reside in the Numbers: Divisibility section. You'll get the concentrated practice you need. If you use our 10-out-of-10-or-nothing training technique (page 2), your accuracy will be honed to the point where you simply don't get questions wrong. An **800** will be within reach.

Note to Users

The CrushTheTest questions are based on our study of hundreds of real SAT questions and we've done our best to mimic their style. Some CrushTheTest questions are like real SAT questions on steroids. These questions (~ 10% of the total) are important practice and are identified in the text by an exclamation mark (!) after the question number.

Note to Parents

Most of the questions are ordinary math problems but there are also motorcycle chases, gambling, vomiting, a break-in, one arrest, and other bits of fun you'll never find in a standard math text. We also take the occasional potshot at our fictional creation: the illustrious Standardized Testing Service (aka STS). All of the math is serious.

The CrushTheTest 10-out-of-10-or-nothing Training Technique

Answers and solutions to each 10-question section are at the back of the book. It is quite tempting to check answers as you work. Resist this. Instead, use the CrushTheTest 10-out-of-10-or-nothing Training Technique.

Step 1

Tear the answer sheet out of the back of the book and give it to someone you trust.

Step 2

Do a 10-question section.

Step 3

Ask the person who has the answer sheet to tell you if you got all 10 questions right. Instruct them NOT to tell you how many you got wrong or which ones.

Step 4

Keep trying until you get 10 out of 10. Like any good training technique, it is <u>difficult</u> and can be <u>frustrating</u>. *Keep trying.* (If you just don't know the math behind a question, learn it and then come back to the question.)

This training technique forces you to KNOW when you are absolutely SURE of an answer. This is the key to what we call "extreme accuracy" and it is what you need for a test like the SAT. It's easy to look at an answer key and say, "oh yeah, now I get it." Don't fall into this trap. Find your mistake the hard way. Do 10-out-of-10-or-nothing. It's nasty, but remember, on the real test, you won't find out about wrong answers until you see your score!

The SAT is a game. Play to win.

A Quick Way to Score ETS* Practice Sections

The math SAT consists of 3 sections with 16, 18, and 20 questions. Do a practice section in *The Official SAT Study Guide* published by the Educational Testing Service (ETS). Answer ALL the questions (wild guessing is break-even under the ETS scoring system). Count how many you got right. Use the table below to estimate your score. For example, if you typically get 1 wrong in each section, you'll probably get a 750 on the real test.

For each section: 3 wrong is a 650
2 wrong is a 700, 1 wrong is a 750.

Score	Number Correct out of 16	Number correct out of 18	Number Correct out of 20
500	9	9	11
550	11	11	13
600	12	13	15
650	13	15	17
700	14	16	18
750	15	17	19
800	16	18	20

Practice Tips

The ETS practice tests in *The Official SAT Study Guide* are precious: they are as close as you are going to get to the real thing. Don't look at an ETS practice section until you are ready to take it. Time yourself strictly. Get your score using the chart above. Switch off between doing untimed CrushTheTest practice and timed ETS practice.

---

* ETS is a registered trademark of Educational Testing Service (ETS). This publication is not endorsed or approved by ETS.

It's Not a Speed Test, You Can't Train For It, and Other Myths

If you gave people enough time to carefully answer all the questions on the SAT, there would be a big cluster of scores between 700 and 800. This would ruin the nice distribution that SAT consumers (*i.e.*, colleges) have come to expect. Of course, you could make the questions harder, give people plenty of time, and still get your precious distribution. But then you would be testing specialized knowledge rather than basic math. So what's the mother of all testing agencies to do? The Educational Testing Service (aka ETS*) could admit that their test has limitations. They could give everyone enough time and not worry about the cluster of high scores . . . okay, sorry — we promise to stay off the hallucinogens. The reality is, of course, any retreat from the speed requirement would ruin everything for the ETS and their customers.

The SAT is an effective means of *artificially* distinguishing between people. The speed requirement produces a nice distribution of scores and the blissfully gullible colleges can then accept someone with a 750 and reject someone with a 650 even though the score difference tells them almost nothing (flipping a coin would spoil the illusion). If you happen to be the creator of the statistically beautiful distribution you state categorically that the test is actually NOT a speed test and do your best to keep a straight face.

Not that the SAT is *entirely* meaningless. The problem-solving on the math part of the test is directly related to what you see in a college-level introductory science or math course. So if you have studied algebra and geometry and you score above 600, you will probably be able to handle introductory math, chemistry, or physics in college. If you don't break 500, stay away from these courses. If you are either a natural test-taker or you are serious about your SAT training and you break 700, smile broadly and take your score to the gullible colleges. Once you're in and you've finished your intro science and math courses you can forget about your SAT score.

---

* ETS is a registered trademark of Educational Testing Service (ETS). This publication is not endorsed or approved by ETS.

The relevance of the verbal part is a harder question. The verbal test would ideally predict a student's ability to understand scholarly work and write readable, thoughtful essays in college. But the ability to speed-read passages and answer ETS-style questions is not directly relevant to any college course. Being able to write a high-scoring ETS essay may likewise be largely useless in college. CrushTheTest is interested in observations, ideally from college professors, about the relevance, if any, of the verbal part of the SAT to college work.

There is some interesting research showing that a person's SAT score can be partially predicted by a *personality* test. The researchers used the Myers-Briggs test and found good correlations between personality profile and SAT score. This kind of research gives you an idea of just how easy it might be to increase your score: all you have to do is mimic the approach of natural test-takers.

Which brings us to Stanley Kaplan. It was Kaplan who proved that large score increases resulting from training were possible. The test-makers (ETS) didn't like it. Training won't help they said. They wanted to believe their test was more than any test could possibly be so they blew off reality, called Kaplan a charlatan, and stuck their heads in the sand. Many years later, the more stubborn ETS officials were dead, Kaplan was a millionaire, and the premier testing organization had quietly reversed itself and was busy marketing its very own prep materials! (No sense letting Kaplan make *all* the money.) It's too much even for ETS to sell prep materials for an "aptitude" test so now they say the letters S-A-T don't stand for anything! The technically correct way to refer to the SAT is to say, "The test formerly known as the Scholastic Aptitude Test, formerly known as the test you can't train for, now known as the test you'd be crazy <u>not</u> to train for."

The test-makers like to pretend otherwise, but the fact is, anyone who starts off getting above 600 on a few practice math tests should aim for an 800. You know the math — what's missing is training. You don't have to be a genius. Remember, all the questions have to be answerable in under two minutes, so there are no truly difficult questions. The mystique of the 800 is just that, a mystique. But it will help you get into college.

Which brings us to those wonderful bureaucrats, the college admissions officers. The well-known limitations of the SAT do not prevent most of them from worshipping the test. The more slippery ones utter platitudes containing the phrase ". . . there are many factors . . ." and go on to make a not-so-honest effort to convince people that the SAT is certainly not being used to arbitrarily cull the admissions pool. They forget that regular people aren't as gullible as college administrators. A few colleges have put their money where their mouth is — they have made the SAT optional. The rest continue to spout their platitudes even though no one is listening.

Since you have to play the game, you might as well win. Your training should focus on 1) **speed**, 2) **accuracy**, and 3) **question recognition** ability. These superficial skills will get you the score you need. Once you've matriculated at the college of your choice, you can concentrate on developing serious skills, gaining deep understanding, and doing creative work . . . and forget about your SAT score.

Speed is developed by highly motivated and disciplined practice. Use the practice tests in the *The Official SAT Study Guide* published by the Educational Testing Service. This material should be reserved exclusively for "dress rehearsal" FOR REAL timed practice. And you should take your score (see page 3 for a scoring shortcut) on each section very seriously.

Accuracy under the time pressure is another matter; ordinary practice won't cut it. You need a hardcore training technique and we think the CrushTheTest 10-out-of-10-or-nothing Training Technique is perhaps a bit brutal but is also just what you need. The technique is described on page 2 – or you can use the CrushTheTest website with LEVEL set to 3 bars. On Level 3, the website insists that you get 10 out of 10 on each section. You are not told which ones you got wrong or even how many you got wrong and you are thereby forced to develop what we call "extreme accuracy." Extreme accuracy is not taught in school. At school, just being probably right is almost always good enough. For the SAT, you have to KNOW when you are right. As you try again and again on a CrushTheTest section, you will begin to develop this skill. If you can get into the "BE SURE" mindset, you will indeed CrushTheTest.

Question recognition is important because, as you know, the test is all about speed. You must IMMEDIATELY characterize a question by type and get on the short route to the answer. CrushTheTest questions are organized in eight main categories: algebra, geometry, units, statistics, numbers, reading, logic, and counting. Each category has 1-4 subcategories so you can concentrate on each particular kind of question asked on the SAT. Each subcategory contains a mix of questions that require a straightforward approach, the stare-at-it-till-you-see-it approach, or the read-it-carefully-three-times approach. We want you to reach the point where every question on the real SAT looks familiar to you.

Remember, the test formerly known as the Scholastic Aptitude Test DOES NOT tell you how smart you are. Even if you get an 800, it doesn't mean you will cure cancer or create the successor to the transistor or figure out how the physical constants of the universe were set to their present values. If you actually are a genius, you are not going to find it out by answering large numbers of cute little tricky questions in a short time. Unfortunately, many people remember their score for decades and still feel strongly about it until the day they die. This is a bizarre result of the system we've created; it's nothing but a fantastic illusion.

Algebra

Warmup

basics, easy, not SAT-like

Manipulation

words-to-equations, rearranging equations, exponents including fractional and negative exponents, square roots, cube roots

Fractions

ratios, proportions, compounding, algebra problems using fractions

Functions

$f(x)$ language, matching graph to $f(x)$, shifting graphs up/down and left/right, intersection points, algebra problems using functions

Word Problems

compounding costs, speed-distance-time problems, words-to-equations-to-solutions, given constraints produce equation or possible answer

Warmup

1. If $x = \dfrac{1}{p}$ then $\dfrac{1}{x} =$

    (A) $p - 1$

    (B) $1 - p$

    (C) p

    (D) $-p$

    (E) p^2

2. If $w = x^a$ and $z = x^b$ then $wz =$

    (A) x^{ab}

    (B) x^{a+b}

    (C) x^{a-b}

    (D) $x^a + x^b$

    (E) $x^{a/b}$

3. The quantity $(ab)^{-5} =$

    (A) $a^5 b^5$

    (B) $\dfrac{a}{b^5}$

    (C) $\dfrac{b}{a^5}$

    (D) $\dfrac{1}{a^5 b^5}$

    (E) 5^{ab}

4. The quantity $\dfrac{xy^2 + y}{y} =$

    (A) xy

    (B) $x(y+1)$

    (C) $xy + 1$

    (D) $y(x+1)$

    (E) $xy - 1$

5. The quantity $\dfrac{x-1}{1-x} =$

    (A) x

    (B) $-x$

    (C) 1

    (D) -1

    (E) cannot be simplified

6. The quantity $x^2 - y^2 =$

    (A) $(x-y)^2$

    (B) $(x+y)^2$

    (C) $\dfrac{x}{y} + \dfrac{y}{x}$

    (D) $(x+y)(x-y)$

    (E) $x^2 + xy + y^2$

7. If $\dfrac{a}{b} = \dfrac{x}{y}$ and $x \neq 0$ then

    (A) $\dfrac{a}{x} = \dfrac{b}{y}$

    (B) $ay = bx$

    (C) $\dfrac{y}{b} = \dfrac{x}{a}$

    (D) $x = \dfrac{ay}{b}$

    (E) all of these

8. If k is a positive number then k percent of x is equal to:

    (A) kx

    (B) $100kx$

    (C) $100k + x$

    (D) $k + 100x$

    (E) $\dfrac{kx}{100}$

9. If y is the result of increasing x by 30 percent then $y =$

(A) $1.3x$

(B) $x + 30$

(C) $x + 0.30$

(D) $0.3x$

(E) $130x$

10. The square root of x cubed is equal to:

(A) x

(B) x^6

(C) x^5

(D) $x^2\sqrt{x}$

(E) $x\sqrt{x}$

End of Section

This page intentionally left blank.

Manipulation

1. Jason rents out his family's house while they are on vacation. He charges y dollars per day for the rental and receives a 20 dollar tip from the renters. Jason's family has five members including Jason, and all of the money Jason receives from the renters including the tip is divided evenly amongst the five family members. Jason spends 6 dollars of his share leaving him with z dollars from the rental venture. Which of the following represents number of days the house was occupied by the renters?

(A) $\dfrac{z}{5y} - 2$

(B) $\dfrac{5z - 14}{y}$

(C) $\dfrac{5z + 10}{y}$

(D) $\dfrac{z + 6}{5y}$

(E) $\dfrac{6z + 20}{5y}$

2. If $9^{b+1} = a^8$ then $27^b =$

(A) $\dfrac{a^{12}}{27}$

(B) $\dfrac{a^{21}}{9}$

(C) $3a^8$

(D) $3a^9$

(E) $3a^{16}$

3. If $x = 2b$ and $a = 3$ then $\dfrac{2^{a-b}}{2^x} =$

(A) 8^{-b}

(B) 8^{b-1}

(C) 8^{1-b}

(D) 8^b

(E) 8

4. If $r + s + t = r - u = s - t$ then which of the following is true?

I. $r = -2t$

II. $s + t + u = 0$

III. $r + 2s = 2(s - t)$

(A) I, only

(B) I and II, only

(C) I and III, only

(D) II and III, only

(E) I, II, and III

5. If $x = \dfrac{ab+c}{a}$ then $xb =$

(A) $xa - c$

(B) $\dfrac{xa - c}{a}$

(C) $x^2 - cx$

(D) $x^2 a - cx$

(E) $\dfrac{x^2 a - cx}{a}$

6. If $x^{\frac{8}{3}} = y^{\frac{6}{7}}$ and $y > 0$ then $x^2 \cdot y^{-\frac{3}{7}} =$

(A) $\sqrt[3]{x}$

(B) $x\sqrt[3]{x}$

(C) $\sqrt[3]{x^2}$

(D) $x\sqrt[3]{x^2}$

(E) $x^2 \sqrt[3]{x}$

7! If $a^2 = b^2 = c^2 = d^2$ then the average of a, b, c, and d expressed in terms of a could be:

(A) $-a$

(B) $2a$

(C) $\dfrac{a}{4}$

(D) $-\dfrac{a}{2}$

(E) none of these

8. If $x + y \neq 0$, for what values of x is the equation below true?
$$2^{|-x-y|} = \dfrac{1}{2^{-x-y}}$$

(A) $x > -y$

(B) $x < -y$

(C) $x > y$

(D) $x < y$

(E) all values of x

9. If $y + 2^{x+2} = 2^{x+3}$ then which of the following expresses $2^{\frac{x+2}{2}}$ in terms of y?

(A) $\dfrac{3y}{2}$

(B) y

(C) $\dfrac{y}{2}$

(D) $\sqrt{y}$

(E) $\dfrac{\sqrt{y}}{2}$

10. If $\dfrac{x+y}{x-y} = a$ and a, x, and y are positive numbers greater than 1 and $y \neq x$ then $y =$

(A) $\dfrac{ax}{a-1}$

(B) $\dfrac{a}{ax+x}$

(C) $\dfrac{ax-x}{a+1}$

(D) $\dfrac{a+1}{ax-x}$

(E) $\dfrac{ax}{a+1}$

End of Section

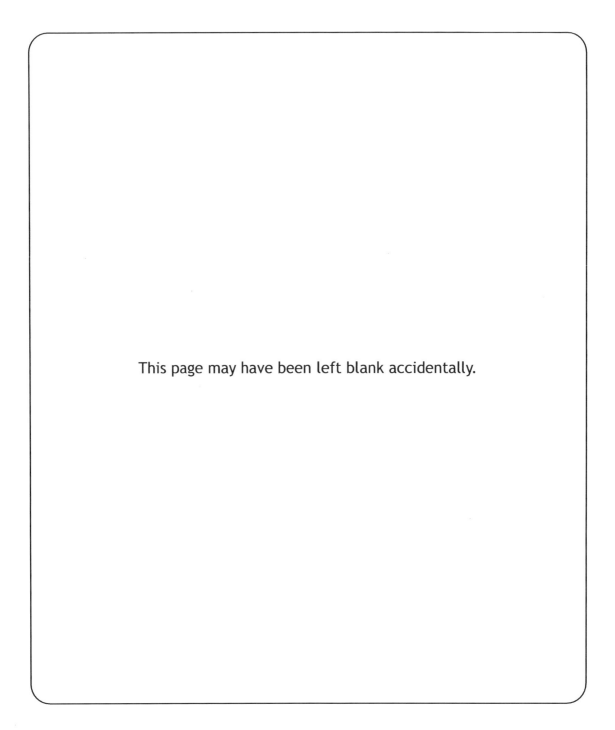

This page may have been left blank accidentally.

Fractions

1. If you pour half of a full small bucket of water into an empty big bucket, the big bucket will be three-tenths full. How many times bigger than the small bucket is the big bucket?

   (A) 1.5

   (B) 1.67

   (C) 3

   (D) 3.33

   (E) 5

2. A small bucket holds 80 percent of the volume of a big bucket. The big bucket is two-thirds full with water. The small bucket is empty. What fraction of the small bucket do you need to fill with water to have just enough liquid to finish filling the big bucket?

   (A) 5/12

   (B) 4/15

   (C) 7/15

   (D) 8/15

   (E) 5/6

Note: Figure not drawn to scale.

3. Rectangle ACDE is twice as long as it is wide. Point B is one-quarter of the way between points A and C. One ant crawls from point B through point A to point E along the edge of the rectangle traveling a total distance of 10 cm. Another ant crawls from point B through points C and D to point E along the edge of the rectangle traveling a total distance of x cm. How far does the second ant travel?

(A) 15.25 cm

(B) 15.33 cm

(C) 15.75 cm

(D) 16.25 cm

(E) 16.67 cm

4. Line segments AC, BC, CD, CE, and BD are shown above. The length of BC is equal to p percent of the length of AC. The length of CD is equal to p percent of the length of CE. If the length of BD is half the length of AC and one-third the length of CE, then what is the value of p?

(A) 10

(B) 20

(C) 30

(D) 40

(E) 50

5. Half of the people who showed up to take the SAT one day at the (fictional) PainIsGood Test Center got nauseous and one-third of the people who got nauseous threw up. One-fifth of the people who did <u>not</u> throw up got bits of vomit on their test papers. One-third of the people with vomit on their test papers decided to leave. All of the people who threw up also left. What fraction of prospective test-takers did <u>not</u> leave?

(A) 2/9

(B) 4/9

(C) 5/9

(D) 2/3

(E) 7/9

6. You have a hundred dollars in dollar bills. You are going to divide it up (unequally) among four people. You want everyone to get a whole number of dollars and you don't want any money left over. To fulfill these conditions, you can divide the money according to which of the following ratios?

I. $4 : 3 : 2 : 1$

II. $10 : 5 : 2 : 1$

III. $9 : 7 : 3 : 1$

(A) I, only

(B) II, only

(C) I and II, only

(D) I and III, only

(E) II and III, only

Note: Figure not drawn to scale.

7! On rectangle ACDE point B is one-quarter of the way between points A and C. A trained ant crawls from point B through point A to point E along the edge of the rectangle traveling 10 cm. A second ant crawls from point B through points C and D to point E along the edge of the rectangle traveling 20 cm. What is the ratio of the length to the width of ACDE?

(A) 1.2

(B) 1.25

(C) 1.33

(D) 1.5

(E) cannot be determined

8. The duration of the lunch break for an executive of the fictional Standardized Testing Service (STS) is directly proportional to the number of years the executive has been with the company. Executive A has been with STS for exactly 5 years and takes 2-hour lunch breaks. The lunch breaks of executive B take a whopping 3 hours and 40 minutes. How long has executive B been "working" for STS?

(A) 7 years, 10 months

(B) 8 years, 4 months

(C) 9 years, 2 months

(D) 10 years, 8 months

(E) 11 years, 6 months

9. If $a^2 - a^2 b^2 + b^2 = 0$ then the expression below must be equal to which of the following quantities?

$$\frac{1}{\frac{1}{a^2} + \frac{1}{b^2}}$$

(A) $\dfrac{1}{4}$

(B) $\dfrac{1}{2}$

(C) 1

(D) 2

(E) 4

10. If $y = \dfrac{1 - x^2}{1 - \frac{1}{x^2}}$ and $x \neq 0, \pm 1$, which of the following must be true?

(A) $\sqrt{y} > 0$

(B) $|y| = -y$

(C) $\dfrac{y}{x} < 0$

(D) $x^2 + y^2 > 1$

(E) none of these

End of Section

Who is SATAN?

SATAN is a fictional character who we imagine writes the SAT. Although some people really do think the SAT is produced deep underground, there is no hard evidence for this so we continue to consider SATAN to be entirely fictional.

SATAN will offer unto you many a false path and these paths shall turn 2 minutes into 20 minutes and thou shalt be burnt. Your sacred task is to learn all of SATAN's tricks so that you may always take the shining path of righteousness rather than the road to Hell.

CrushTheTest questions are NOT real SAT questions; instead, a single CrushTheTest question is designed to lay before you the diabolical traps that you might encounter in two or three real level 4 or 5 SAT math questions.

So when we say "SATAN does this" or "SATAN does that" we mean on the real SAT whose end-of-each-section viciousness is here simulated and sometimes even magnified by your friendly CrushTheTest angels.

That's right. We're the good guys who know how to pretend to be the bad guys and who even know how to be badder bad guys than the real bad guys.

Welcome to CrushTheTest.

Functions

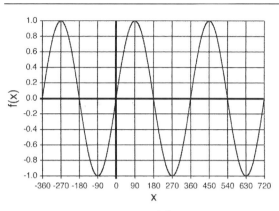

1. The function $y = f(x)$ is shown above. Which diagram represents the function $y = 2f(x+90)+2$?

(A)

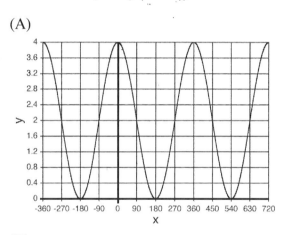

(B)

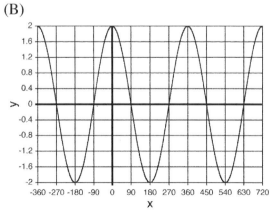

(C)

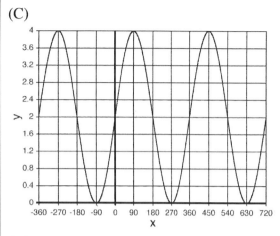

(D)

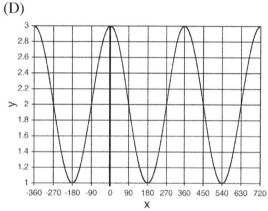

(E)

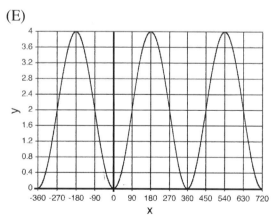

2. If $g(x)$ is a quadratic function of x, which of the diagrams below could be the graph of $f(x)$ given by:

$$y = f(x) = g(x) \cdot (x^3 + 5x^2 + 6x) \text{?}$$

(A)

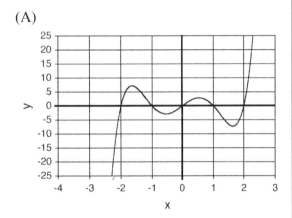

(B)

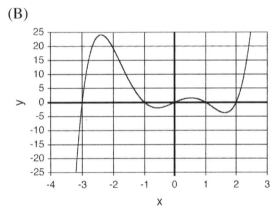

(C)

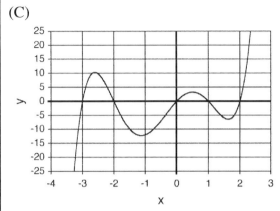

(D)

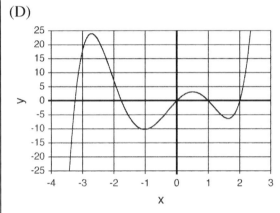

(E)

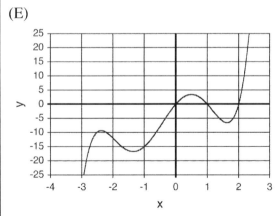

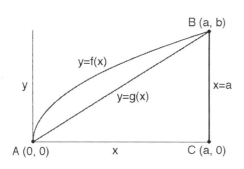

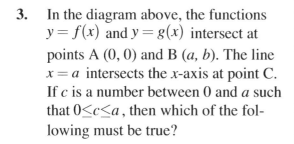

3. In the diagram above, the functions $y = f(x)$ and $y = g(x)$ intersect at points A $(0, 0)$ and B (a, b). The line $x = a$ intersects the x-axis at point C. If c is a number between 0 and a such that $0 \leq c \leq a$, then which of the following must be true?

    I. $f(c) - g(c) \geq 0$

    II. $f(a/2) > g(c)$

    III. The area of $\triangle ABC > \dfrac{c \cdot f(a)}{2}$

    (A) I, only

    (B) II, only

    (C) I and II, only

    (D) II and III, only

    (E) I and III, only

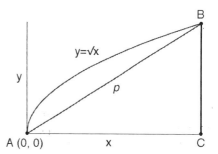

Note: Figure not drawn to scale.

4. In the diagram above, line p intersects the curve $y = \sqrt{x}$ at point B and line BC is perpendicular to line AC. The length of line segment AB is $\sqrt{6}$. What is the area of triangle ABC?

    (A) $\sqrt{2}$

    (B) $2\sqrt{2}$

    (C) $\sqrt{3}$

    (D) $2\sqrt{3}$

    (E) cannot be determined

5. If $f(x) = x^2 + x + 2$ then which of the equations below has the same solution set as $f(x+2) = 4$?

(A) $x^2 + 5x + 2 = 0$

(B) $x^2 + 5x + 4 = 0$

(C) $x^2 + 5x + 6 = 0$

(D) $x^2 + 3x + 2 = 0$

(E) $x^2 + 3x + 6 = 0$

6. If $f(x) = 4x^2 + 6$ for what value of x does $\dfrac{f(x)}{2} = f(2x)$?

(A) 0

(B) $\dfrac{3}{14}$

(C) $\sqrt{\dfrac{3}{14}}$

(D) $-\sqrt{\dfrac{3}{14}}$

(E) none of these

7. A line with positive slope m intersects the curve $y = x^2 - 2$ at two points with coordinates (a, b) and $(3, c)$. If $a<0$ which of the following contains three possible values of the slope m?

I.   1.5, 2.5, 3.5

II.   1, 2, 3

III. 2, 4, 6

(A) none

(B) I, only

(C) II, only

(D) III, only

(E) I, II, and III

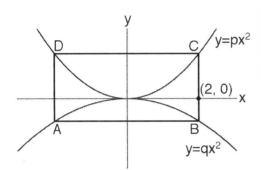

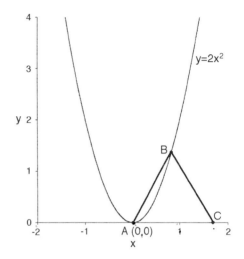

8. Two curves, $y = px^2$ and $y = qx^2$ intersect rectangle ABCD at its four corners. Which of the following expressions gives the area of the rectangle?

(A) $4(p+q)$

(B) $8(p+q)$

(C) $16(p+q)$

(D) $8(p-q)$

(E) $16(p-q)$

9! The curve $y = 2x^2$ intersects equilateral triangle ABC at vertex A $(0, 0)$ and at vertex B. What is the area of the triangle?

(A) $\sqrt{3}$

(B) $3\sqrt{3}$

(C) $\dfrac{3\sqrt{3}}{2}$

(D) $\dfrac{3\sqrt{3}}{4}$

(E) cannot be determined

10. An expensive car containing a number of (fictional) STS executives and their mistresses is moving along a country road at constant speed. The driver is drunk and hits a tree causing the car to stop suddenly (there are several minor injuries and one arrest). Which distance (x) vs. time (t) graph best represents the motion of the car?

(A)

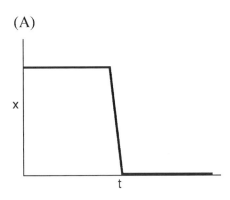

(B)

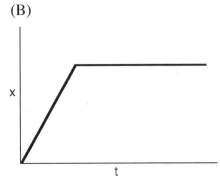

(C)

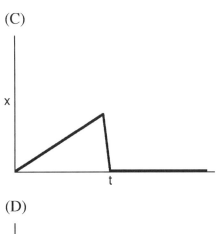

(D)

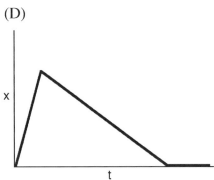

(E)

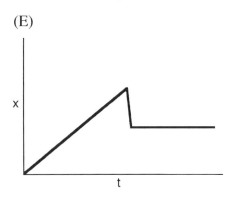

End of Section

Who is David Owen?

Word Problems

1. Bob and Carol and Ted and Alice are backpacking in the wilderness. Each person carries *x* pounds of equipment. "Equipment" does not include food, so the total weight of equipment (4*x*) is constant. During the first night, Bob sneaks 10 pounds of equipment from his pack into Carol's. Ted and Alice each sneak 7 pounds of equipment from their packs into Carol's. Later, when the other three are picking berries, Carol divides all the equipment in her pack evenly amongst the packs of her three pals. If Bob's pack now contains 54 pounds of equipment, how much did it contain originally?

    (A) 32 pounds

    (B) 35 pounds

    (C) 40 pounds

    (D) 42 pounds

    (E) 45 pounds

2. The area of a triangle is 10 square inches. By how many square inches does the area of the triangle increase if the height is increased by 2 inches while the length of the base remains unchanged?

    (A) 4

    (B) 5

    (C) 10

    (D) 12

    (E) cannot be determined

3. Your new motorcycle has a top speed that is 20% faster than the top speed of your old motorcycle. On your old motorcycle it takes you two hours to get to your friend's house traveling at the top speed of the bike (and risking your life for the thrill of speed). How many <u>minutes</u> does the trip take at the top speed of your new motorcycle? Assume, in each case, that you manage to travel at the top speed of the motorcycle for the whole trip (no stop signs, traffic lights *etc.*).

(A) 100

(B) 96

(C) 95

(D) 92.5

(E) 90

4. After breaking into the headquarters of the fictional Standardized Testing Service (STS) and erasing all their hard drives thereby bringing about a 2-year hiatus from standardized tests, Joe – a fictional hero – is escaping on his motorcycle. Unfortunately, there are a number of fictional, heavily armed STS thugs 10 miles behind him riding specially-built bikes going 150 miles per hour. They are NOT planning to arrest him. If Joe can make it another 50 miles before they catch up to him, he will be able to cross a bridge that will not hold the STS bikes. What minimum average speed in miles per hour must Joe maintain over the next 50 miles to reach the bridge just in the nick of time?

(A) 115

(B) 117.5

(C) 120

(D) 122.5

(E) 125

5. When the width and length of a rectangle are each reduced by 20%, the area of the new rectangle is 12 units less than the area of the original rectangle. What is the area of the original rectangle?

(A) $12\frac{1}{2}$

(B) 15

(C) $33\frac{1}{3}$

(D) 45

(E) 60

6. Square A has an area 30 square meters larger than square B. The perimeter of square A is 8 meters larger than the perimeter of square B. The length in meters of one side of square A is:

(A) 6.5

(B) 7.5

(C) 8.5

(D) 9.5

(E) 10.5

7. The average of two numbers is x. If you multiply one of the numbers by 18, the average of the two new numbers (one of which is unchanged) is $2x$. What is the ratio of the smaller original number to the larger original number?

(A) 1/15

(B) 1/16

(C) 1/18

(D) 1/20

(E) 1/21

8. Grandma driving her old car can make it from her house to Las Vegas in 8 hours. If she borrows your car and drives like a maniac, she can make the same trip in 6 hours. Her average speed for the trip in your car is 35 miles per hour faster than her average speed for the trip in her car. What average speed in miles per hour does grandma attain driving your car from her house to Las Vegas?

(A) 95

(B) 105

(C) 125

(D) 130

(E) 140

9. In one month Alice-the-lawyer earns half of what her husband, Bill-the-artist, earns in a year (12 months). Together, the happy couple earns 168,000 dollars per year. What is Alice's monthly income in dollars?

   (A) 12,000

   (B) 10,000

   (C) 8,000

   (D) 4,000

   (E) 2,000

10. When Einstein was a small boy, he used to like to blow bubbles. All the bubbles he blew were either big or small. Little Albert always blew his bubbles so that the number of big bubbles was exactly equal to one more than the square root of the number of small bubbles. For one particular bubble-blowing session, the total number of bubbles little Albert blew might have been which of the following? (There is no evidence Einstein ever actually did anything this pointless.)

   (A) 42

   (B) 43

   (C) 44

   (D) 45

   (E) 46

   End of Section

David Owen, author of *None of the Above: The Truth Behind the SATs*,[2] is not what you'd call a fan of the Educational Testing Service (ETS). Owen's book was originally published in 1985 and was updated in 1999. Most of the dirt is from the early 80's.

The ETS may have cleaned up its act by now . . . anything is possible.

The following pages let you taste some of the dirt.

None of the Above is well worth reading in its entirety if for no other reason than the fact that the whole sordid affair (ETS vs. reality) is extremely amusing especially if your sense of humor has a dark side.

If the antics of ETS don't make you ROFL, you will still gain something important: the complete transformation of your understanding of the role of testing in education (and in your life!).

The founder of Princeton Review, John Katzman, called Owen's work "The best book ever written about the SAT."

We tend to agree.

Geometry

Lengths, Angles, Perimeters

circles, regular polygons, sum of angles, parallel lines, triangles, similar triangles, right triangles, algebraic perimeters, symmetry

Areas

inscribed circles, inscribed triangles, inscribed squares, shaded regions, symmetry, sectors of circles

Triangles

symmetry, possibility problems (length, angles, areas), 30-60-90, 45-45-90, isosceles triangles, equilateral triangles, inscribed equilateral triangles

Points and Space

xy coordinates, possible areas, lines that form figures, possible distances given constraints (locus problems), mental rotations and manipulations

Lengths, Angles, Perimeters

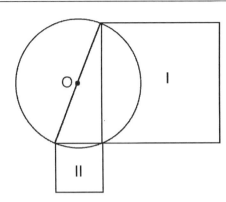

1. The area of circle O is 20π. The sum of the areas of square I and square II is:

   (A) 60

   (B) 80

   (C) 90

   (D) 120

   (E) cannot be determined

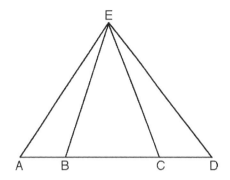

Note: Figure not drawn to scale.

2. In the figure above, AE=DE and BE=CE. The area of triangle AED is 5 times the area of triangle BEC. What is the ratio of the length of AB to the length of BC?

   (A) 0.5

   (B) 0.67

   (C) 1

   (D) 2

   (E) cannot be determined

3! Line *l* is tangent to circle O at point (*a*, *b*) and *a*>0 and *b*>0. If the center of circle O is at the origin and if circle O consists of all points (*x*, *y*) such that $x^2 + y^2 = 10$, which of the following expressions gives the *y*-intercept of line *l*?

(A) $\dfrac{10}{b}$

(B) $\dfrac{10a}{b}$

(C) $\dfrac{10b}{a}$

(D) $\dfrac{10+a}{b}$

(E) $b - \dfrac{10a}{b}$

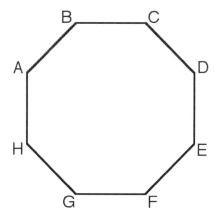

4. Regular octagon ABCDEFGH has sides of length *s*. What is the length of line segment AD (not shown) in terms of *s*?

(A) $s\sqrt{2}$

(B) $s(\sqrt{2}+1)$

(C) $s\sqrt{3}$

(D) $s(\sqrt{3}+1)$

(E) $s\sqrt{3}/2$

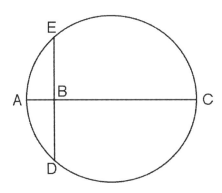

Note: Figure not drawn to scale.

5.   In the diagram above, AC is a diameter of the circle, AB=2, BC=8, and DE is perpendicular to AC. What is the length of DE?

   (A) 4

   (B) 6

   (C) 8

   (D) 10

   (E) cannot be determined

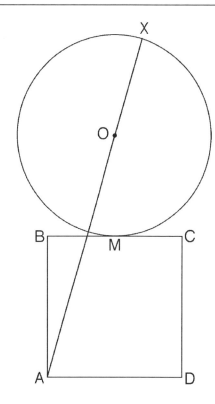

6.   In the diagram above, circle O has a diameter of 20. Line segment BC is tangent to circle O at point M and M is the midpoint of BC. If ABCD is a square and if line segment AB has length 14, what is the length of line segment AX?

   (A) $35 + \sqrt{2} \approx 36.4$

   (B) 36

   (C) $34 + \sqrt{3} \approx 35.7$

   (D) $34 + \sqrt{2} \approx 35.4$

   (E) 35

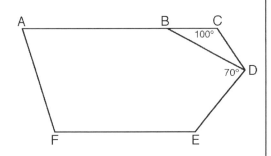

Note: Figure not drawn to scale.

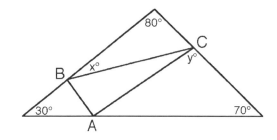

Note: Figure not drawn to scale.

7. In the figure above, AC is parallel to EF, BC=CD, angle BCD=100°, and angle BDE=70°. What is the measure in degrees of angle FED?

    (A) 120

    (B) 130

    (C) 140

    (D) 150

    (E) 160

8. In the figure above, $\triangle ABC$ is a right triangle with $AB = \sqrt{2}$, $AC = \sqrt{6}$. If $y = 100 - x$, what is the value of x?

    (A) 25

    (B) 30

    (C) 35

    (D) 40

    (E) cannot be determined

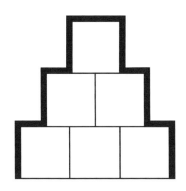

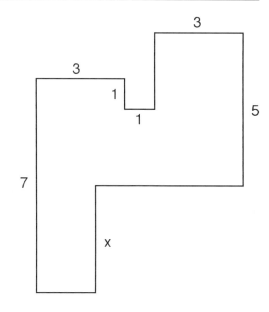

9! The child of an STS executive builds a pyramid out of N identical cubical blocks ($N = 6$ is shown). The child says "Daddy, daddy, the outside edge of the front face of my pyramid [shown in bold] measures 300 cm and each of my blocks has a volume of 125 cubic cm; guess how many blocks are in my pyramid!" The STS executive has no idea but he saves the question for a future test. What is the value of N?

(A) 91

(B) 120

(C) 136

(D) 210

(E) 465

10! If all line segments in the figure shown above are either vertical or horizontal, which of the following gives the perimeter of the figure in terms of x?

(A) $28 + x$

(B) $29 + x$

(C) $30 + x$

(D) $25 + 2x$

(E) $26 + 2x$

End of Section

ETS Dirt I

Owen tells us that on the 1926 SAT:

> "The analogy section contained 40 items and students were given six minutes [as in 360 seconds] to complete them all."[3]

That's 9 seconds per analogy.

The bell curves must have been absolutely beautiful!

You would also get a beautiful bell curve if you told people to hit a button as soon as they saw a light flash red and then graphed their response times.

Areas

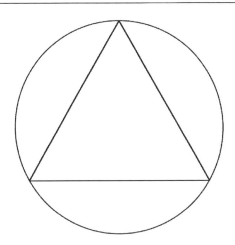

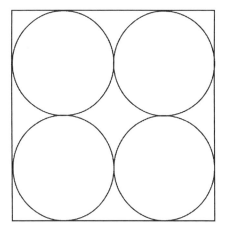

1. An equilateral triangle is inscribed in a circle with radius 2. What is the area of the triangle?

(A) $3\sqrt{3}$

(B) $2\sqrt{3}$

(C) $3\sqrt{2}$

(D) $\pi\sqrt{6}$

(E) $\pi\sqrt{10}$

2. The area of the square in the diagram is equal to s^2. The four circles have equal radii and are tangent to each other and to the sides of the square. What fraction of the area of the square is occupied by the four circles?

(A) $\dfrac{\pi s^2}{4}$

(B) $\dfrac{6\pi s^2}{\sqrt{3}}$

(C) $\dfrac{2\pi}{5}$

(D) $\dfrac{\sqrt{6}\pi}{6}$

(E) $\dfrac{\pi}{4}$

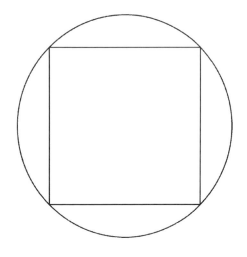

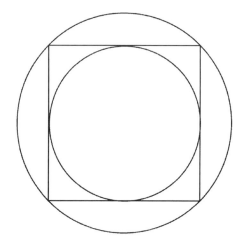

3. A square is inscribed in a circle. The area of the circle is 6. What is the area of the square?

(A) 4

(B) 16/π

(C) 12/π

(D) 3√2

(E) 8/π

4. A square is inscribed in a large circle. A small circle is inscribed in the square. If the area of the small circle is 1, what is the area of the large circle?

(A) √2

(B) 3/2

(C) √3

(D) 2

(E) 2√2

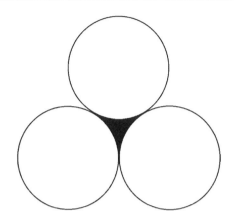

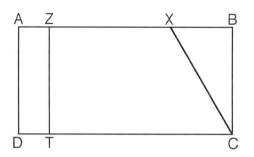

5. Each circle in the figure above has radius $r=1$. What is the area of the shaded region surrounded by the three circles?

(A) $\dfrac{3\sqrt{3} - \pi}{2}$

(B) $\dfrac{2\sqrt{3} - \pi}{3}$

(C) $\dfrac{3\sqrt{2} - \pi}{2}$

(D) $\dfrac{2\sqrt{3} - \pi}{2}$

(E) $\dfrac{3\sqrt{3} - \pi}{3}$

6. In the figure above, ZX/AB = 4/7. If the area of rectangle AZTD is equal to the area of triangle BCX and if the area of quadrilateral AXCD = 30, what is the area of rectangle ABCD?

(A) 34

(B) 35

(C) 36

(D) 37.5

(E) 38.5

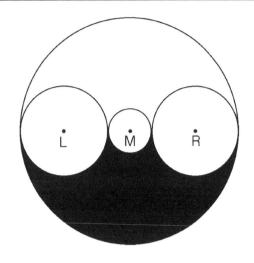

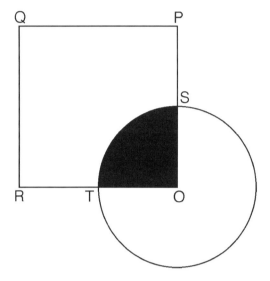

7. The largest and smallest circles in the diagram are concentric with center M. Circles L and R are tangent to the smallest circle and to the largest circle and each has a radius equal to twice the radius of the smallest circle. Line segment LMR lies on the diameter of the largest circle. The area of the shaded region is 16π. What is the radius of the smallest circle?

(A) 1

(B) $\sqrt{2}$

(C) 2

(D) $2\sqrt{2}$

(E) 3

8. The center of circle O is one of the vertices of square OPQR. The midpoint of OP is S and the midpoint of OR is T. The shaded region occupies what fraction of the square?

(A) $\dfrac{\pi\sqrt{2}}{20}$

(B) $\dfrac{\pi\sqrt{3}}{36}$

(C) $\dfrac{\pi}{12\sqrt{2}}$

(D) $\dfrac{\pi}{16}$

(E) $\dfrac{\pi}{20}$

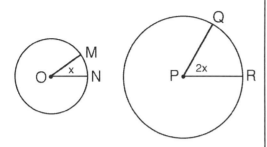

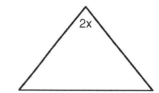

Note: Figure not drawn to scale.

Note: Figure not drawn to scale.

9. The area of circle P is twice that of circle O. The measure of angle MON is equal to x. The measure of angle QPR is equal to $2x$. If the clockwise distance along circle O from point M to point N is equal to 3, what is the clockwise distance along circle P from point Q to point R?

(A) 6

(B) $6\sqrt{2}$

(C) $6\sqrt{3}$

(D) 12

(E) 24

10! An isosceles triangle has vertex angle $x<90°$ and an area equal to 2. A new isosceles triangle is drawn with vertex angle $2x$. If the new triangle has the same height as the original triangle, the area of the new triangle is:

(A) $2\sqrt{2}$

(B) $2\sqrt{3}$

(C) 4

(D) 6

(E) cannot be determined

End of Section

ETS Dirt II

Here's a great quote from Owen's book:

> "ETS claims, somewhat incredibly, that the SAT is 'relatively un-speeded' . . ." (Owen cites ETS literature).[4]

Relatively unspeeded? Surely they must be joking.

Speed is the single most important factor in breaking 700. See our article beginning on page 4 for the truth according to CrushTheTest about speed and its importance to ETS.

For the full quote from Owen's book about ETS' infamous "relatively unspeeded" comment, see note #4 in the References and Notes section.

Triangles

1. What is the largest possible area in square cm of a right triangle whose hypotenuse measures 6 cm?

   (A) 8

   (B) 9

   (C) 12

   (D) 15

   (E) 18

2. In triangle ABC, AB is chosen as the base. The height of the triangle with AB as the base is h and h=AB. Which of the following is true?

   I. $\triangle$ABC could be a right triangle.

   II. Angle C cannot be a right angle.

   III. Angle C could be less than 45°.

   (A) none

   (B) I, only

   (C) I and II, only

   (D) I and III, only

   (E) I, II, and III

3. If triangle XYZ is not a right triangle then a line drawn from vertex Z to side XY that is perpendicular to XY is <u>always</u>:

(A) longer than XY

(B) shorter than XY

(C) longer than XZ and longer than YZ

(D) shorter than XZ and shorter than YZ

(E) none of these

4. The length of each of the sides of a triangle is a positive integer and n is a positive integer. If the length of one side is $n+10$ and the length of another side is $n+12$, then the <u>shortest</u> possible length of the third side is:

(A) $n-2$

(B) $n+2$

(C) $n+11$

(D) 2

(E) 3

5. A line segment is drawn from the origin to point A (4, 3). Another line segment is drawn perpendicular to the first from point A to point B (*b*, 0) on the *x*-axis. What is the value of *b*?

(A) 6.25

(B) 6.33

(C) 6.5

(D) 6.67

(E) 6.75

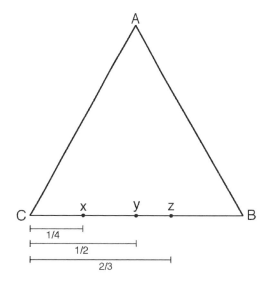

6. Triangle ABC is equilateral and BC=1. Another equilateral triangle is to be inscribed in ABC so that each side of triangle ABC contains one vertex of the inscribed triangle. Which of the three points along BC in the figure may be used as a vertex of the inscribed equilateral triangle?

(A) *y*, only

(B) *y* and *z*, only

(C) *x* and *z*, only

(D) *x* and *y*, only

(E) *x*, *y*, and *z*

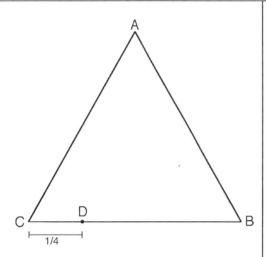

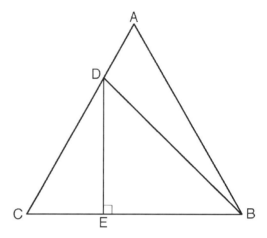

Note: Figure not drawn to scale.

7. Triangle ABC is equilateral and BC=1. A line segment is to be drawn from point D to AC. If the line segment intersects AC at point E, what is the shortest possible length of DE?

(A) $\dfrac{1}{8}$

(B) $\dfrac{1}{4}$

(C) $\dfrac{1}{2}$

(D) $\dfrac{\sqrt{3}}{4}$

(E) $\dfrac{\sqrt{3}}{8}$

8. Triangle ABC is equilateral. If BE=DE and DE is perpendicular to BC, what is the ratio of the length of CE to the length of BC?

(A) $\dfrac{1}{3}$

(B) $\dfrac{1}{4}$

(C) $\dfrac{1}{\sqrt{3}}$

(D) $\dfrac{1}{\sqrt{3}+1}$

(E) $\dfrac{1}{\sqrt{3}+\sqrt{2}}$

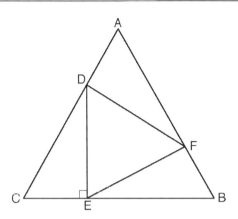

Note: Figure not drawn to scale.

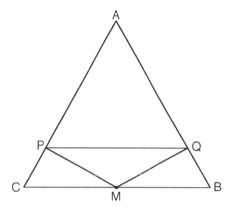

Note: Figure not drawn to scale.

9. Triangle ABC is equilateral. If triangle DEF is also equilateral and DE is perpendicular to BC, what is the ratio of the length of CE to the length of BC?

(A) $\dfrac{1}{3}$

(B) $\dfrac{1}{4}$

(C) $\dfrac{1}{\sqrt{3}}$

(D) $\dfrac{1}{\sqrt{3}+1}$

(E) $\dfrac{1}{\sqrt{3}+\sqrt{2}}$

10! Triangle ABC is still equilateral. If M is the midpoint of BC and MP and MQ are perpendicular to AC and AB, what is the ratio of the length of PQ to the length of BC?

(A) $\dfrac{1}{3}$

(B) $\dfrac{3}{8}$

(C) $\dfrac{2}{3}$

(D) $\dfrac{3}{4}$

(E) cannot be determined

End of Section

ETS Dirt III

Here's a question from a 1981 SAT reproduced for us in Owen's book:[5]

Which row contains both the square of an integer and the cube of a different integer?

(A)   7, 2, 5, 4, 6

(B)   3, 8, 6, 9, 7

(C)   5, 4, 3, 8, 2

(D)   9, 5, 7, 3, 6

(E)   5, 6, 3, 7, 4

High school student Michael Galligan pointed out to ETS that TWO of the answer choices were correct.

Can you find the two correct answers?

Points and Space

1. A rectangular prism measures 3 cm by 4 cm by 5 cm. Points A and B are different points on the surface of this solid. What is the largest possible length of line segment AB?

   (A) $4\sqrt{2}$ cm (≈ 5.7 cm)

   (B) $\sqrt{41}$ cm (≈ 6.4 cm)

   (C) $5\sqrt{2}$ cm (≈ 7.1 cm)

   (D) $2\sqrt{15}$ cm (≈ 7.7 cm)

   (E) $6\sqrt{3}$ cm (≈ 10.4 cm)

2. What is the area of the triangle formed by the x-axis, the line $y = x$, and the line $y = -\frac{1}{2}x + 3$?

   (A) 3

   (B) 6

   (C) 9

   (D) 12

   (E) 15

3!   A rectangle has a perimeter of 20 inches. Which of the following could be the area of this rectangle in square inches?

I.   8

II.   23

III.   26

(A)   I, only

(B)   II, only

(C)   I and II, only

(D)   II and III, only

(E)   I, II, and III

4.   Points A and B on plane P are 5 units apart. How many points in plane P are <u>both</u> 3 units from point B <u>and</u> 6 units from point A?

(A)   0

(B)   1

(C)   2

(D)   3

(E)   4

5. Points A and B on plane P are 5 inches apart. How many points in plane P are 4 inches from point B and <u>more than</u> 4 inches from point A?

(A) 0

(B) 1

(C) 2

(D) 3

(E) more than 3

6. Points A and B are 6 inches apart. Point M is the midpoint of AB. Point C is 4 inches from point M and point D is 2 inches from point B. Points A, B, C, D, and M all lie on a plane. Which of the following could be the distance between points C and D in inches?

I. 0

II. 1

III. 9

(A) none

(B) I, only

(C) II, only

(D) I and II, only

(E) I, II, and III

7. Points A, B, C, and D lie on a plane. The distance between points A and B is 24, AC=BC=15, and AD=BD=13. Which of the following could be the length of CD?

I.   4

II. 9

III. 14

(A) II, only

(B) III, only

(C) II and III, only

(D) I and III, only

(E) I and II, only

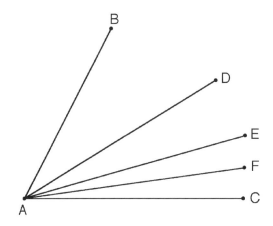

8. In a the diagram above, line segment AD bisects angle BAC, line segment AE bisects angle DAC, and line segment AF bisects angle EAC. Angle BAC is less than 90 degrees. If all angles less than 90 degrees and greater than 0 degrees in the diagram are measured, including overlapping and non-overlapping angles, how many numerically different results will be obtained?

(A) 10

(B) 9

(C) 8

(D) 7

(E) 6

red	pink
blue	gray

9. The card represented above is painted a different color in each of four quadrants as shown. It is rotated $x°$ counter-clockwise about an axis perpendicular to the plane of the card and passing through its center. Which of the cards below could NOT represent the result of this rotation?

(A)
blue	red
gray	pink

(B)
pink	gray
red	blue

(C)
gray	pink
blue	red

(D)
gray	blue
pink	red

(E)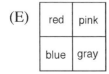
red	pink
blue	gray

10. A cube has a different letter on each face. The letters are A, B, C, D, E, and F. Another cube is similar except that the letters on the faces are A, B, C, G, H, and I. Both cubes are opaque. The cubes are glued together face-to-face and set down on an opaque table. If the cubes are not moved, what is the <u>minimum</u> number of <u>different</u> letters that must be visible to a person who walks around the table? (The person can see all of the exposed faces.)

(A) 5

(B) 6

(C) 7

(D) 8

(E) 9

End of Section

ETS Dirt IV

Both (B) and (C) were correct on the Galligan question above.

Choice B (3, 8, 6, 9, 7) contains the square of 3 and the cube of 2 and 3 and 2 are different integers.

But choice C (5, 4, 3, 8, 2) contains the square of -2 and the cube of 2 and -2 and 2 are also different integers.

ETS re-scored thousands of tests: the most twisted argument in the world will not allow ETS to shout down a math mistake so they had little choice.

It's an ironic mistake because, to this day, ETS loves to trick students into forgetting that integers include negative numbers.

Units

Prices, Percents, 2D, 3D

compound interest, markups/markdowns, rpm's, algebraic percents, surface area, volume, volume unit conversions, scale of maps

Algebra

given algebraic quantities combine to get another quantity, percents, rates, speeds

Prices, Percents, 2D, 3D

1. A politician puts $1,000 into an account at Bank of Anything For You (BOAFY) that earns 50% interest per year. If no withdrawals are made, approximately how much money will be in the account at the end of four years?

   (A) $4,000

   (B) $5,000

   (C) $6,000

   (D) $8,000

   (E) $10,000

2. Another politician makes an initial deposit of $1,000 at BOAFY. Every year the amount of money in the account increases by x percent. No money is withdrawn. After 10 years there is $12,000 in the account. Which equation is correct?

   (A) $1 + \dfrac{12x}{100} = 10^{12}$

   (B) $1 + \dfrac{10x}{100} = 12^{10}$

   (C) $1 + \left[\dfrac{x}{100}\right]^{10} = 12$

   (D) $\left[\dfrac{x+1}{100}\right]^{10} = 12$

   (E) $\left[1 + \dfrac{x}{100}\right]^{10} = 12$

3. Joe-the-sucker has $32 left after playing a gambling game in which you are guaranteed to lose exactly one-third of your money every time you play. Joe played 5 times before he wised up. The first time he played, he played with all the money in his pocket. Each time after the first time, he played with whatever money he had left. How much money did Joe start with?

(A) $160

(B) $162

(C) $243

(D) $333

(E) $441

4. An unscrupulous store wants to have a Christmas sale in which everything is marked 20% off. However, they don't want to actually reduce any of their prices. So, early in November, they <u>mark up</u> everything in the store by x percent so that when they take 20% off the day after Thanksgiving, everything will be back to its original price. What is x?

(A) 10

(B) 15

(C) 20

(D) 25

(E) 30

5. Farmer Brown divided his k acre farm into two parcels, A and B. Parcel A was $\frac{1}{3}k$ acres and he sold x percent of it. He sold y percent of parcel B. What percent of the whole farm was sold?

(A) $\dfrac{100(x+2y)}{k}$

(B) $\dfrac{100(x+2y)}{3k}$

(C) $\dfrac{x+2y}{3k}$

(D) $\dfrac{x+2y}{3}$

(E) $\dfrac{x+3y}{2}$

6. The radius of each of the 4 tires on a car is 30 cm. If the car travels at 72 km per hour, how many revolutions per minute are made by each tire? (1 km=1000 meters; 1 meter=100 cm)

(A) $\dfrac{2000}{\pi}$

(B) $\dfrac{1000}{\pi}$

(C) $\dfrac{500}{\pi}$

(D) $\dfrac{250}{\pi}$

(E) $\dfrac{200}{\pi}$

7. The inside of a small hollow cube has a total surface area of 24 square centimeters. A larger hollow cube has inside edges that measure 8 centimeters in length. Wanda drills a hole in the top face of each cube. She fills the small cube with water and then pours the water from the small cube into the large cube without spilling. Wanda repeats this process until the large cube is filled with water. How many times (total) does Wanda fill the small cube with water?

(A) 8

(B) 27

(C) 64

(D) 125

(E) 216

8! The sum of the lengths of all the edges of a cube is equal to p cm. The surface area of the cube is equal to a square cm. Which of the following must be FALSE?

(A) $a = \sqrt{p}$

(B) $a = p$

(C) $a = p^2$

(D) $a = p^3$

(E) $a = p^4$

9. A one liter can of paint is used by the legendary Peter the Perfect Painter to perfectly cover exactly 100 square feet of non-porous wall perfectly evenly. All the paint is used. Approximately how thick in <u>millimeters</u> is the layer of paint?
(1 liter = 1000 cubic centimeters; 1 inch = 2.5 centimeters (approx.); 1 centimeter = 10 millimeters)

(A) 0.1

(B) 0.2

(C) 0.25

(D) 0.5

(E) 1.0

10. A right circular cylinder has a lateral area of a square inches and a volume of v cubic inches. If $a = v = x$, what is the value of x?

(A) 1

(B) $\sqrt{2}$

(C) 2

(D) $2\sqrt{2}$

(E) cannot be determined

End of Section

ETS Dirt V

Math mistakes are hard to squirm out of. Verbal mistakes are a different story. Here's a question taken from an SAT administered in 1980 and reproduced in Owen's book:[6]

> Unfortunately, certain aspects of democratic government sometimes put pressure on politicians to take the easy way out, allowing _____ to crowd out _____.
>
> (A)   exigencies . . necessities
>
> (B)   immediacies . . ultimates
>
> (C)   responsibilities . . privileges
>
> (D)   principles . . practicalities
>
> (E)   issues . . problems

We love this question.

Before you tear your hair out over it, we should tell you that Owen tried this question on a number of successful, highly-regarded, professional writers: none thought there was one correct answer and one said flat out she would have chosen the "wrong" answer.

The writing in this question is really terrible — none of the answers makes a well-written sentence. In our opinion, the answer chosen by ETS is the 4th (!) best answer.

What do you think?

ETS did not re-score the test containing this question.

Algebra

1. It takes G gallons of water to fill 6 hot-tubs. If you have N gallons of water but use 80% of it to water the lawn, how many hot-tubs can you fill using the remaining water?

(A) $\dfrac{6N}{5G}$

(B) $\dfrac{6G}{5N}$

(C) $\dfrac{30N}{G}$

(D) $\dfrac{6GN}{5}$

(E) $\dfrac{5GN}{6}$

2. Joe (an SAT connoisseur) decides chocolate covered cockroaches would go well with the test so he plans to sneak some in for his 8th attempt at a 2400. He can buy n cockroaches for d dollars. The price per cockroach is independent of the number of roaches purchased. How much will it cost in dollars for Joe to buy n^3 chocolate covered cockroaches?

(A) $\left(\dfrac{d}{n}\right)^3$

(B) d^3

(C) $n^2 d$

(D) $\dfrac{d}{n^3}$

(E) d^2

Units: Algebra

3. Hoping to miss her scheduled SAT at the PainIsGood test center, Lily drives one third of the distance to the test center at 30 miles per hour (mph), one third of the distance at 20 mph, and the final third at 15 mph. She does annoy the other drivers but does not miss the test. What is Lily's average speed for her agonizing trip to the test center?

(A) 15 mph

(B) 17.5 mph

(C) 20 mph

(D) 21.67 mph

(E) 24 mph

4. One Super Lube Dude can do x oil changes per year. The lovely town of Carsville has y cars. If all oil changes are performed at Super Lube and all cars get exactly 3 oil changes per year, how many Super Lube Dudes are needed to take care of all the cars in Carsville?

(A) $3xy$

(B) $\dfrac{3y}{x}$

(C) $\dfrac{3x}{y}$

(D) $\dfrac{x}{3y}$

(E) $\dfrac{1}{3xy}$

5. Every time a question is answered incorrectly or left blank by someone taking the SAT, SATAN laughs with delight and Hell gets hotter. The rate of temperature increase in Hell is d degrees for every x questions NOT answered correctly. One year, N people took the SAT and the average test-taker answered p percent of Q questions correctly. By how many degrees did Hell get hotter that year due to the SAT?

(A) $\dfrac{dNQ}{x}\left(1-\dfrac{p}{100}\right)$

(B) $dNQx\left(1-\dfrac{p}{100}\right)$

(C) $dNQx(100-p)$

(D) $\dfrac{NQpx}{100d}$

(E) $\dfrac{dNQp}{100x}$

6. In Piano City, there are n pianos that are each tuned exactly once a year. There are t piano tuners in the city. A tuner is paid d dollars for every 5 pianos tuned. What is the average income in dollars per year earned by a tuner for tuning pianos in Piano City?

(A) $\dfrac{dnt}{5}$

(B) $\dfrac{5d}{nt}$

(C) $\dfrac{dn}{5t}$

(D) $\dfrac{5dt}{n}$

(E) $\dfrac{5nt}{d}$

7. A bicycle has two wheels each with radius r meters. Ryder rides the bicycle five times around a circular track with radius R meters. How many rotations are made by each wheel?

    (A) R / r

    (B) $5R / r$

    (C) $2\pi r / (5R)$

    (D) $5R / (2\pi r)$

    (E) $5\pi R / r$

Questions 8-10: Some college students who have trouble adjusting to "daily life without mommy" respond by drinking alcohol until they vomit. The technical term used by mental health professionals to refer to this behavior is "stupid." The technical term for people who drink <u>more than</u> six ounces of liquor <u>per hour</u> at a party is "moronic." People who are moronic are not considered stupid (they are beyond stupid) although they may vomit.

8. There were x moronic people at a party out of a total of N people. Thirty percent of the people who were not moronic were stupid. What percent of the people at the party were stupid?

    (A) $30 \left(1 - \dfrac{x}{N}\right)$

    (B) $70 \left(1 - \dfrac{x}{N}\right)$

    (C) $\dfrac{30N + 70x}{N}$

    (D) $0.3(N + x)$

    (E) $0.7(N + x)$

Questions 8-10: Some college students who have trouble adjusting to "daily life without mommy" respond by drinking alcohol until they vomit. The technical term used by mental health professionals to refer to this behavior is "stupid." The technical term for people who drink <u>more than</u> six ounces of liquor <u>per hour</u> at a party is "moronic." People who are moronic are not considered stupid (they are beyond stupid) although they may vomit.

9. At a party, there were x stupid people and y moronic people and $x + y = 72$. All 72 vomited and 20 of them lost consciousness (passed out). The number of unconscious morons was 4 times the number of unconscious stupid people. Ten percent of stupid people passed out. What percent of moronic people passed out?

   (A) 40

   (B) 50

   (C) 60

   (D) 75

   (E) 90

10. At a party with N people, there were no moronic people. One third of the people at this party didn't drink any alcohol. There were x bottles of hard liquor at the party each containing y ounces of liquor. If the party lasted 3 hours, what is the maximum number of bottles that could have been consumed at the party?

    (A) $12Nx / y$

    (B) $12N / y$

    (C) $6N / y$

    (D) $6Ny / x$

    (E) $6Nx / y$

    End of Section

ETS Dirt VI

Here is the full analysis of the "certain aspects of democratic government" verbal SAT question above.[7]

Nicholas von Hoffman is a professional political writer. He said the item was "so poorly constructed" that it couldn't be answered. A, B, C, or E were all possible answers according to him.

The well-known journalist William F. Buckley called the "correct" answer "an awful case of Sunday-suited English."

Stephen R. Graubard, former professor of history at Harvard, at Brown and editor of the journal of the American Academy of Arts and Sciences when Owen interviewed him, also said there were multiple answers: "I don't think questions of this sort ought to be asked."

Owen called John Simons, professor of English at Colorado College. Simons was an SAT essay exam grader at the time. He picked A, B, *and* E saying, ". . . it seems impossible to argue that there is one right answer . . ."

Next was Elizabeth Hardwick, novelist, author of *Bartleby in Manhattan* (a collection of literary essays), and advisory editor for *The New York Review of Books*. The ETS answer was "not good English usage," and she would call "reasonable" any of the choices except for C. "Everything considered, I would have answered D," she said.

Andrew Hacker, professor of political science at Queens College, couldn't decide between B and E: "I would have wasted so much time on this question that my final score would have been quite dismal."

We think Ms. Hardwick had the best argument: D is the best answer, E and A are both possible, B is poor usage, and C doesn't work.

Amazingly, ETS said the one correct answer was B. According to Owen, SAT verbal sections are full of questionable questions.[8]

Statistics

Warmup

mean, median, mode basic definitions (not SAT-like)

Averages

changes in average, possible values given average, algebra problems involving averages, average of a combined group, average as a constraint

Probability

get P given ratios, get P given numbers, express P in terms of x, dual probabilities, get P from counting, applications of P (statistical surveys and studies)

Mean, Median, Mode

comparison of mean and median, possibilities given constraints, algebraic word problems based on MMM, effect of changes to set on MMM of the set

Warmup

1. The median of 10, 10, 10, 10, 10 is:

   (A) 0

   (B) 5

   (C) 10

   (D) 50

   (E) there is no median

2. The median of 2, 8, 8, 12 is:

   (A) 2

   (B) 8

   (C) 12

   (D) 10

   (E) 5

3. The median of 2, 2, 3, 7, 9 is:

   (A) 2

   (B) 3

   (C) 7

   (D) 5

   (E) 2.5

4. The median of 2, 2, 3, 100 is:

   (A) 2

   (B) 3

   (C) 100

   (D) 51.5

   (E) 2.5

5. The median of 2, 2, 2, 6 is:

   (A) 2

   (B) 6

   (C) 4

   (D) 3

   (E) there is no median

6. The mode of 2, 8, 8, 12 is:

   (A) 2

   (B) 8

   (C) 12

   (D) 10

   (E) 5

7. The mode of 2, 5, 9, 11 is:

(A) 2

(B) 5

(C) 9

(D) 11

(E) all of these

8. The mode of 2, 2, 8, 8, 10 is:

(A) 2

(B) 8

(C) 10

(D) 2 and 8

(E) there is no mode

9. The median of 1, 2, 3, 50, 50, 70, 80 is:

(A) 30

(B) 40

(C) 50

(D) 60

(E) 70

10. Which of the following is true of the set of four numbers a, b, c, d?

(A) b>a

(B) the median is (b+c) / 2

(C) d>a

(D) a ≠ d

(E) none of these

End of Section

Averages

1. In a typical day at the TSA (Testing School of America), Sally takes five tests. Her score on the first test is x. On each test after the first, her score is 4 points lower than her score on the previous test. What is her average score for all five tests?

   (A) $x - 8$

   (B) $x - 10$

   (C) $x - 12$

   (D) $x - 15$

   (E) $x - 16$

2. Sally is scheduled to take her Nth test at the TSA. She has an average of A for her first $N-1$ tests. She is finally fed up and doesn't bother to show up for the Nth test. She receives a zero for this test. How many points lower than A is Sally's average for all N tests?

   (A) $\dfrac{A}{N}$

   (B) $\dfrac{A}{N-1}$

   (C) $\dfrac{AN}{N-1}$

   (D) $\dfrac{A(N-1)}{N}$

   (E) $\dfrac{A}{N(N-1)}$

3. The average of four positive numbers is 70. Which of the following is true?

   I.   If one number is 60, one number must be 80.

   II. At least one number is greater than 70.

   III. The largest number cannot be 300.

   (A) none
   (B) I and II, only
   (C) II, only
   (D) III, only
   (E) II and III, only

4. The average of five positive integers is 50. One of the five integers is 26. The largest possible value of one of the other four numbers is:

   (A) 212
   (B) 215
   (C) 218
   (D) 221
   (E) 224

5. The average of a, b, c, and d is equal to y and the value of d is 12 less than the value of y. The average of a, b, and c must be:

(A) 12 more than y

(B) 8 more than y

(C) 6 more than y

(D) 4 more than y

(E) 3 more than y

6. One group of people (group I) has an average height of 62 inches. Another group (group II) has an average height of 70 inches. The average height of <u>all</u> the people in both groups together is 67 inches. If there are 120 people in group I, how many are in group II?

(A) 45

(B) 72

(C) 75

(D) 180

(E) 200

7. Jack is an independent contractor working for a radioactive isotope production company. Jack earns 30 dollars per hour for routine checks and 45 dollars per hour for work in radioactive areas. On one particular day he earns d dollars for routine checks and another d dollars for work in a radioactive area. He doesn't take any breaks. What is the average number of dollars per hour (dollars earned divided by hours worked) Jack earns that day?

(A) 35

(B) 36

(C) 37.5

(D) 38.5

(E) cannot be determined

8. The average of a and b is x. The average of a, b, c, and d is $1.5b$. If $a/b = 3$, what is the average of c and d?

(A) $0.25x$

(B) $0.5x$

(C) $0.75x$

(D) x

(E) $1.25x$

9. The set of different integers a, b, c, and d has an average equal to x. The average of a^2, b^2, c^2, and d^2 is equal to y. Which of the following statements must be true?

I. $y > 2$

II. $y = x^2$

III. $y > x$

(A) none

(B) I, only

(C) II, only

(D) III, only

(E) I, II, and III

10! The average of 5 different integers is 20. The largest of the 5 integers is 23. The smallest of the five integers is N. How many possible values of N are there?

(A) 3

(B) 4

(C) 5

(D) 6

(E) more than 6

End of Section

ETS Dirt VII

Here's a scary quote from Owen's book:

> "James McMenamin, director of admissions at Columbia, told me that 'any experienced reader of applications at a selective college is going to be suspicious, at this point, about any big jump in scores.' "[9]

Recently, ETS changed its policies and they now allow "score choice" which means you can send only your scores from your best overall test or, if you want, you can send scores from more than 1 test date.

HOWEVER, Columbia is still in the dark ages — they have rejected "score choice" — they insist on seeing ALL scores NOT just the scores you want to send. Presumably, they still penalize you for any big jumps. Cornell, Stanford, and Yale are also "all scores" colleges.

Harvard, Haverford, MIT, Princeton, Reed, and most other colleges allow you to choose to send only your scores from your best SAT test date AND they say if you send scores from more than one test date, they will consider your *highest scores in each section* from all the times you took the test.

You can find the full list of colleges and their official "all scores" vs "highest section scores" policies on the college board website (www.collegeboard.com).

Or ask matt@crushthetest.com for the score choice pdf.

ETS says on their website that they implemented score choice to "make the SAT experience a little less stressful." This is the kind of thing that warms my heart on a cold, blustery day.

Of course, it is *possible* the ETS decision may have had something to do with the fact that the SAT's main competitor, the ACT, allows score choice AND has been steadily gaining market share.

Probability

1. A bag has blue, green, and yellow marbles. There are 3 times as many green marbles as yellow marbles and 4 times as many blue marbles as green marbles. What is the probability of randomly selecting a yellow marble?

   (A) 1/16

   (B) 1/15

   (C) 1/12

   (D) 1/8

   (E) 1/7

2. A bag contains N marbles. A marble selected at random from the bag could be one of m different colors. There are x ($x > 1$) marbles of each color in the bag. What is the minimum number of marbles you must select at random from the bag in order to be 100% certain you will have (outside the bag) a pair of marbles of the same color?

   (A) $\dfrac{N}{m} + 1$

   (B) $m + 1$

   (C) $mx + 1$

   (D) $x + 1$

   (E) $\dfrac{N}{mx} + 1$

3. Another blue, green, and yellow marble bag. The probability of picking a blue marble is 1/2. The probability of picking a green marble is 1/3. There are twenty yellow marbles in the bag. Which of the following is true about this bag of marbles?

I. There are 40 blue marbles.

II. There are 30 green marbles.

III. The probability of picking a yellow marble is 1/5.

(A) none

(B) I, only

(C) II, only

(D) III, only

(E) I, II, and III

4. Yet another bag. Same colors. There are twice as many green marbles as yellow marbles. The probability of picking a blue marble is 4/5. The number of green marbles is x. What is the number of blue marbles?

(A) $15x$

(B) $12x$

(C) $7.5x$

(D) $6x$

(E) $4x$

5. The evil blue, green, and yellow marble bag has an equal number of blue and green marbles. There are four times as many yellow marbles as blue marbles. Some marbles are solid and some are hollow. For each color, there are five times as many solid marbles as hollow marbles. What is the probability of randomly choosing a solid green marble?

(A) 7/20

(B) 5/36

(C) 4/27

(D) 4/25

(E) 2/15

6. A slightly more interesting bag with blue, green, and yellow marbles has some marbles that explode when removed from the bag. Only blue marbles explode. There are 162 blue marbles in the bag, not all of which explode. Two-thirds of the marbles in the bag are blue. If one marble is chosen at random from the full bag, the probability that it will explode is 1/9. What is the ratio of exploding blue marbles to all blue marbles?

(A) 2/27

(B) 2/9

(C) 1/9

(D) 1/6

(E) 1/3

7. If the probability of picking a yellow marble out of a bag is $1/n$ and n is an integer greater than 1, what is the ratio of the number of yellow marbles in the bag to the number of other marbles?

(A) $\dfrac{1}{n}$

(B) n

(C) $\dfrac{n}{n-1}$

(D) $\dfrac{1}{n-1}$

(E) $\dfrac{1}{n+1}$

8. All of the numbers from 1 to 100 inclusive are written in a single line. If you choose a digit at random from the line of digits, what is the probability that you would choose a 1?

(A) 1/8

(B) 3/20

(C) 4/35

(D) 5/48

(E) 7/64

9. A randomly-selected group of people were asked the following question: "Do you think the average high school principal could run a successful business?" The results were as follows: 240 people said NO; 100 people said MAYBE; 20 people said YES. Based on this survey, if you asked another 90 randomly-selected people the same question, how many people would be expected to say NO?

(A) 45

(B) 60

(C) 72

(D) 75

(E) 80

10. According to one study, the probability that an American adult ate too much sugar as a child is 80%. According to a companion study, 30% of people who ate too much sugar as children have trouble controlling their weight as adults while only 10% of people who did not eat too much sugar as children have a weight control problem. According to both studies, how many American adults out of 100 would be expected to have trouble controlling their weight?

(A) 20

(B) 22

(C) 24

(D) 26

(E) 28

End of Section

ETS Dirt VIII

Bowdoin is a highly selective college in Maine. They do not require the SAT. They dropped the requirement because they discovered that the majority of people who did really well at Bowdoin actually hadn't done particularly well on the SAT. Here's the quote from Owen's book:

> "ETS did not take kindly to its [Bowdoin's] optional SAT policy. 'Bowdoin can make whatever decisions it wants,' Arthur Kroll [an ETS executive] told me somewhat snippily when I asked him in 1983 if he thought Bowdoin was irresponsible not to require the SAT. 'I certainly wouldn't classify them as irresponsible.'
>
> Kroll went on to say that the SAT helped colleges weed out in advance students who probably wouldn't be able to hack it and that 'there's not that much benefit in admitting a lot of people who are going to end up flunking out.' But if the SAT helps colleges do that, I said, isn't Bowdoin being just the teeniest bit irresponsible in not requiring it?
>
> 'It depends on what their goals are,' he said. 'They may not have a goal of maximizing every student's educational performance at Bowdoin. Bowdoin may care less as to whether all students in fact benefit from that experience. But if that was their goal, then I would say that they were being irresponsible.'
>
> There, I'm glad he got that off his chest. But it's been nearly 30 years since the plan went into effect, and Bowdoin hasn't had to auction off its dormitories yet. Its academic reputation is still as high as it used to be."[10]

You have to admire the ETS guy. He could not only spout nonsense like a pro — he had apparently reached the point where he believed it himself!

Mean, Median, Mode

1. A set of four numbers a, b, c, and d has mean x and median y. Which of the following must be true?

I. $x \neq y$

II. $y \neq a$

III. $x < 4y$

(A) none

(B) I and II, only

(C) I and III, only

(D) II and III, only

(E) I, II, and III

2! Four positive numbers a, b, c, and d have mean x and median y. If $a < b < c < d$ then which of the following could be true?

I. $x < y/2$

II. $y = b$

III. $x > c$

(A) I, only

(B) II, only

(C) III, only

(D) I and III, only

(E) II and III, only

3. A set consists of an odd number of integers with mean x, median y, and mode z. If z is a single mode (there are no other numbers with as many multiple occurrences as z), then which of the following is always true?

I. x is an integer

II. y is an integer

III. z is an integer

(A) II only

(B) III, only

(C) II and III, only

(D) I and III, only

(E) I, II, and III

4. Three integers a, b, and c have a median that is two more than the mean. If $a<b<c$ and $a=2$ and $c=12$, then what is the median?

(A) 3

(B) 4

(C) $\dfrac{16}{3}$

(D) 8

(E) 10

5. Four numbers a, b, c, and d have a median that is equal to the average. If $a<b<c<d$, then which statement is true?

(A) $b-a=d-c$

(B) $c+d=2(a+b)$

(C) $d=4a$

(D) $a+c=b+d$

(E) none of these

6. A set of N consecutive integers has average A and median M. What is $M-A$?

(A) 0

(B) 0.25

(C) 0.5

(D) 1

(E) cannot be determined

7. The first member of a set of N integers ($N>2$) is 1. Each member of the set after the first is equal to twice the previous member. Which of the following must be true of the set?

   I.   The mean is greater than the median.

   II. The median is an integer.

   III. The mean is an integer.

(A) I, only

(B) II, only

(C) III, only

(D) I and II, only

(E) I, II, and III

8. Five consecutive positive integers are represented by v, w, x, y, and z in order from smallest to largest. If you replace v with double its value which of the following must be true about the new set of five integers?

   I.   The mean will be larger than x.

   II. The median will be equal to x.

   III. The median will be equal to y.

(A) I, only

(B) II, only

(C) III, only

(D) I and II, only

(E) I and III only

9. A set contains four numbers. The numbers are represented by x, $4x$, $5x$, and $5x-2$. The set contains three different numbers and one pair of equal numbers. Which of the following is <u>possible</u>?

   I.   The mode is x.

   II. The mode is $4x$.

   III. The mode is $5x$.

  (A) III, only

  (B) I and II, only

  (C) I and III, only

  (D) II and III, only

  (E) I, II, and III

10. Two of the numbers in a set of 9 positive numbers are changed. As a result of these changes, the median of the set *decreases* and the mean of the set *increases*. Which of the following changes could have this result?

  (A) double the highest number and halve the second highest

  (B) double the highest number and double the lowest number

  (C) double the highest number and double the second highest

  (D) double the highest number and halve the lowest number

  (E) none of these

End of Section

ETS Dirt IX

Owen gathered evidence that the verbal part of the SAT was being put together by people with very limited writing ability who were basically just flipping through dictionaries. He got his hands on documents showing the ETS development process from the inside as they were part of a legal proceeding and could not be hidden.

Here's a good one:[11]

Games and athletic contests are so intimately a part of life that they are valuable _____ the intensity and vitality of a given culture at any one time.

(A)   modifiers of

(B)   antidotes to

(C)   exceptions to

(D)   obstacles to

(E)   indices of

The test-writers were apparently aware that "intensity of a culture" is a meaningless phrase. Owen points out that saying a "given" culture "at any one time" is nothing but padding, that "intimately a part of life" is an awkward phrase, and that athletics actually do modify culture. He thinks the SAT question above is the product of amateurs:

"In defense of this item Ed Curley [one of the writers] and his colleagues might haughtily imply that they had delved more deeply into its nuances than any layman could ever hope to. But the confidential test reviews prove that ETS's test-makers are hardly the sophisticated scientists they pretend to be. Their trademarks are flabby writing, sloppy thinking, and a disturbing uncertainty about the meanings of shortish words." [12]

OUCH!

Numbers

Divisibility

prime numbers, factors, prime factors, algebraic factors, exponents

Characteristics

positive or negative or fraction, absolute value, odd, even, roots, exponents

Remainders

properties, possible values, applications, modulus, determining from limited information

Digitology

digits in simple math problems, digits in integers, digits in decimals, using bases

Divisibility

1. The integer n is a factor of the integer x and $x > n > 1$. Which of the following must be true?

I. n is a factor of $x + 15n$

II. 5 is a factor of $x + 15n$

III. x is a factor of $x + 15n$

(A) none

(B) I, only

(C) II, only

(D) II and III, only

(E) I, II, and III

2. The positive integer x is a product of three different prime numbers, p, q, and r. If $r > q > p$, which of the following must be true?

I. The greatest prime number that is a factor of x is r.

II. If $p > 5$ then x is not divisible by 5.

III. x^2 is divisible by p, q, and r.

(A) III, only

(B) I and II, only

(C) I and III, only

(D) II and III, only

(E) I, II, and III

3! If h, j, and k are prime numbers and $h = 2$ and $x = hjk + 1$ then which of the following is true?

(A) x is divisible by k

(B) x is divisible by 3

(C) x cannot be prime

(D) x must be prime

(E) none of these

4! If p is a prime number and Q, k, and n are positive integers greater than one and the equation $k^2 n + p^2 = Qkn$ is true, then which of the following must be true?

(A) $Q = p$

(B) $k = n$

(C) $kn < p^2$

(D) $kn > p^2$

(E) $Q = p + 2$

5. If k and n are positive integers greater than 1 and $n \cdot (k - 6n) = 11$, what is the value of k?

(A) 67

(B) 66

(C) 65

(D) 64

(E) 63

6. If j and k are positive integers and $j > k$ and both j and k are divisible by 2, 3, and 5, then the quantity $(j - k)$ must be greater than or equal to:

(A) 15

(B) 30

(C) 45

(D) 60

(E) 65

7. If j and k are positive integers and $j > k$ and both j and k are divisible by 2, 3, and 8, then the quantity $(j - k)$ must be greater than or equal to:

(A) 8

(B) 16

(C) 24

(D) 48

(E) 56

8. The quantity 12^{100} is NOT divisible by which of the following?

(A) 18

(B) 24

(C) 27

(D) 30

(E) 36

9. If positive integer N is the product of 3 different prime numbers and if p is the largest prime factor of N, which of the following must be true?

I. $p > \sqrt[3]{N}$

II. $\dfrac{N}{p^2}$ is NOT an integer

III. $\dfrac{N^2}{p}$ is NOT an integer

(A) none

(B) I, only

(C) II, only

(D) I and II, only

(E) II and III, only

10. If p and n are positive integers and Q is a prime number greater than 3 such that $p^2 - n^2 = 3Q$, then which equation correctly relates the value of Q to the value of n?

(A) $Q = n + 4$

(B) $Q = n + 5$

(C) $Q = 2n + 3$

(D) $Q = n^2 - n + 5$

(E) $Q = -n^2 + 5n + 1$

End of Section

ETS Dirt X

In the late 1970's ETS wanted to prove that the SAT was not coachable. They claimed that practicing the test and learning about it wouldn't help you get a higher score. They apparently actually believed this.

ETS itself commissioned a study of coaching. A guy named Lewis Pike took a bunch of students and taught them as best he could how to take the math part of the test. He didn't really know what he was doing (he was trying coaching for the first time) but, unfortunately for ETS, he made an honest effort. He found that he could increase students' scores on the math section by an average of about 100 points. ETS was not pleased. According to Owen:

> "One ETS executive accused Pike of being a traitor to the company — although he later asked discreetly whether Pike would be willing to give his daughter a little help preparing for the SAT."[13]

Pike followed up his first study with another one that also concluded the test was coachable. Then here's what happened:

> "A few weeks later, Lewis Pike was fired. The following year, the College Board issued a new official statement on coaching, published under this headline: 'Board reaffirms its position that coaching for the SAT is not likely to improve students' scores.' "[14]

ETS claimed Pike's job was eliminated as a result of downsizing. Owen goes on to document the efforts by ETS to suppress the results of its own study.[15]

Characteristics

1. If $x^3 < x < x^2$ then

    (A) $0 < x < 1$

    (B) $1 < x < 2$

    (C) $-1 < x < 0$

    (D) $x < -1$

    (E) $x > 2$

2. If $x < x^3 < x^2$ then

    (A) $0 < x < 1$

    (B) $1 < x < 2$

    (C) $-1 < x < 0$

    (D) $x < -1$

    (E) $x > 2$

3! If $x > y$ and $x \neq 0$ and $y \neq 0$ then

    (A) $x^2 > y^2$

    (B) $\dfrac{1}{x} > \dfrac{1}{y}$

    (C) $\dfrac{1}{x} < \dfrac{1}{y}$

    (D) $x^3 > y^3$

    (E) none of these

4! If $x + 2y > 2x - 3y$ then which of the following is true?

  I. $\dfrac{x}{y} < 5$

  II. The value of x could be greater than the value of y.

  III. If $y < 0$ then $x < 0$.

    (A) II, only

    (B) III, only

    (C) I and II, only

    (D) II and III, only

    (E) I and III, only

5. If $r < s < t$ ($r \neq 0$, $s \neq 0$, $t \neq 0$) then which of the following must be true?

I. $rs < st$

II. $\left|\dfrac{1}{r}\right| > \left|\dfrac{1}{s}\right|$

III. $s^2 > r$

(A) none

(B) I, only

(C) II, only

(D) III, only

(E) I and III, only

6. If $y = \left|\dfrac{1}{2-x}\right|$ and $x \neq 2$ then y increases when:

(A) x increases from 100 to 102

(B) x decreases from -100 to -102

(C) x decreases from 2.3 to 2.1

(D) x decreases from 1.7 to 1.5

(E) x decreases from 0 to -2

7. If a is an integer and $b = a^3$ then which of the following could equal $\sqrt{b}$?

(A) 27

(B) 21

(C) 15

(D) 9

(E) 3

8. If positive integers x and y are both odd and positive integer z is even then which of the following is true?

I. x^z is even

II. $y^z + y^x$ is odd

III. $3 \cdot z^x$ is odd

(A) none

(B) I, only

(C) I and II, only

(D) II and III, only

(E) I and III, only

9. If j and k are integers and $2j + 4 = 4k$ then which of the following must be true?

   I. j is even

   II. k is even

   III. $j \cdot k$ is even

   (A) I, only
   (B) II, only
   (C) III, only
   (D) I and III, only
   (E) II and III, only

10. If x, y, z, and w are positive integers and $xw + yz + yw + xz$ is odd then which of the following is true?

    I.   If x is odd then y is even.

    II. $xyzw$ is odd.

    III. $(x + w)$ is even.

    (A) none
    (B) I, only
    (C) II, only
    (D) III, only
    (E) I, II, and III

    End of Section

ETS Dirt XI

Stanley Kaplan made millions increasing the scores of countless students. He made ETS very unhappy. They were so anti-coaching that they accused students with large score increases of cheating! Here are some examples from Stanley Kaplan's autobiography, *Test Pilot*.

> "One student wanted to attend my classes so badly he came to me on the sly against his parents wishes. He said they didn't understand how competitive it was to get into college in the 1960's and he secretly enrolled in my classes with money he had earned as a paperboy. He increased his SAT score 340 points after taking my course and was accepted to a highly selective college in upstate New York. Today he has a Ph.D. in physics and is a scientist at Xerox corporation."[16]

This guy wasn't investigated but in other cases . . .

> "One Kaplan student was required to retake the SAT because the ETS was suspicious of his 350-point improvement. Guess what? He improved even more . . . Another Kaplan student in Chicago improved her score by 600 points (!) and was retested by ETS with a proctor watching [just her and the proctor] . . . her score was 20 points higher on the retest [total improvement = 620 points], and she was featured on the ABC television show 20/20."[17]

In 2004, Alexis Martin increased her score by 380 points (there were 2 sections back then: math and verbal). ETS invalidated her score. ETS said her low score on the experimental section proved she was cheating off someone who had a different experimental section but the same test otherwise.

There's one experimental section on every SAT. ETS calls it the "variable section." According to Owen, properly-trained test-takers routinely identified and blew off the experimental section in the 1980's (it is difficult or impossible to do this today — such is the nature of an arms race).[18]

Remainders

1! If n and k are positive integers greater than 1 and $4kn + 6k + 2$ is divided by $6k$ which of the following could be the remainder?

I. 1

II. $4k$

III. $2k + 2$

(A) none

(B) I, only

(C) II, only

(D) III, only

(E) I, II, and III

2. The remainder when N is divided by 70 is 58. If today is Monday, what day will it be N days from now?

(A) Monday

(B) Tuesday

(C) Wednesday

(D) Thursday

(E) Friday

3. If n is divided by 90, the remainder is 1. What are the remainders, respectively if $n+179$ and $n+182$ are each divided by 90?

    (A) 89 and 3

    (B) 89 and 2

    (C) 0 and 3

    (D) 0 and 2

    (E) 2 and 3

4. If $n = 5^{50}$ how many different remainders result when n, $n+7$, $n+18$, $n+21$, $n+29$, and $n+32$ are each divided by 11?

    (A) 3

    (B) 4

    (C) 5

    (D) 6

    (E) 7

5. When positive integer n is divided by 5, the remainder is x. When $2n$ is divided by 5, the remainder is y. Which pair (x, y) is not possible?

(A) $(2, 4)$

(B) $(0, 0)$

(C) $(4, 3)$

(D) $(3, 1)$

(E) $(3, 2)$

Questions 6-8: The modulus is defined as follows: $j \bmod k = R$ where R is the remainder when positive integer j is divided by positive integer k.

6. If $j \bmod k = R$ which statement is true for any j and k?

(A) $0 \le R \le j - 1$

(B) $R \ge k - 1$

(C) $R \ge j - 1$

(D) $0 \le R \le k - 1$

(E) $k - 1 \le R \le j - 1$

Questions 6-8: The modulus is defined as follows: $j \bmod k = R$ where R is the remainder when positive integer j is divided by positive integer k.

7. If $j \bmod k = R$ and $j < k$ then

    (A) $R = j$

    (B) $R = k$

    (C) $R = k - j$

    (D) $R = k + j$

    (E) $R = 0$

8. If $j \bmod k = R$ and $k < j < 2k$ then

    (A) $R = j$

    (B) $R = k$

    (C) $R = j - k$

    (D) $R = j + k$

    (E) $R = 0$

9. A positive integer N is divided by 23 and the remainder is 11. What is the remainder if $4N$ is divided by 23?

(A) 11

(B) 15

(C) 19

(D) 21

(E) 22

10. A positive integer that gives a remainder of 5 when divided by 6 and a remainder of 1 when divided by 3 is called a "6-5-3-1" number. How many 6-5-3-1 numbers below 100 are there?

(A) 0

(B) 1

(C) 2

(D) 3

(E) 4

End of Section

ETS Dirt XII

Here's what the College Board and ETS used to say about coaching (from Kaplan's book, *Test Pilot*):

> "If the College Board's tests can be beaten through coaching, then the Board is itself discredited."[19]

But students continued to seek coaching and companies like Kaplan's proliferated and grew and the College Board intoned that it was:

> "appalled by the subversive effect of these commercial enterprises on the goals of education."[20]

They said further that education had become:

> "unwillingly corrupted in some schools to gain ends which we believe to be not only unworthy, but, ironically, unattainable."[21]

Horrors.

(Maybe if the ETS people had taken a prep course they would have learned enough to know that "unwillingly" in this context is incorrect. They meant "unwittingly.")

BTW, *Test Pilot* is also well worth reading. Kaplan is retired now: his memoir is well-written, personal, and honest — you can almost smell what it was like to be there as the nonsense that you couldn't prep for the SAT was being swept away. The sea change is a testament to Kaplan's extraordinary personal abilities and to the power of truth itself.

Kaplan, incidentally, sees significant value in tests like the SAT — everyone takes the same test, so the "playing field" is level.[22] Nevertheless, he spent years mixing it up with ETS.

Digitology

AA + BB ――― BBC	AB + B ――― BA

1. In the correctly worked addition problem above, A, B, and C represent digits. What digit does C represent?

(A) 0

(B) 1

(C) 4

(D) 6

(E) 9

2. In the correctly worked addition problem above, A and B represent digits. What is A?

(A) 5

(B) 6

(C) 7

(D) 8

(E) 9

3! The sum of 185 consecutive positive integers is equal to N. The units digit of N is equal to u. Assuming the sum can start with any positive integer, how many possible values of u are there?

(A) 1

(B) 2

(C) 5

(D) 9

(E) 10

4. If a and b are positive integers such that $a > b > 0$ and the units digit of the product ab is 2, then which of the following could be the units digit of the difference $a - b$?

(A) 2

(B) 3

(C) 6

(D) 8

(E) none of these

5! The sum of a two-digit integer x and another two-digit integer y is divisible by 10. The values of the two integers are such that $9<x<y<100$. The integer x may be represented by AB where A is the tens digit of x and B is the units (ones) digit of x. Similarly, y may be represented by CD where C is the tens digit of y and D is the units (ones) digit of y. Which of the following must be true?

I. If A+B = 8 then D-A = 2.

II. The number of possible values of x is 84.

III. The smallest possible value of y is 20.

(A) I, only.

(B) II, only.

(C) I and III, only.

(D) II and III, only.

(E) I, II, and III.

6. The sum of the digits of a four-digit number x is equal to N. Which of the following could be the sum of the digits of $2x$?

I. N

II. $N - 12$

III. $N + 10$

(A) none

(B) I and II, only

(C) I and III, only

(D) II and III, only

(E) I, II, and III

7. If x and y are numbers and A and B represent digits and $\dfrac{1}{x} = 0.0B$ and $\dfrac{1}{y} = 0.00A$, what is $\dfrac{Bx}{Ay}$?

(A) 100

(B) 10

(C) 1

(D) 0.1

(E) 0.01

8. If Q and R are integers and A and B represent digits and

$$\frac{1}{Q} = 0.0A \text{ and } \frac{1}{R} = 0.0B$$

then one possible value of the product of A and B is:

(A) 6

(B) 12

(C) 15

(D) 18

(E) 20

9. In an alphabetic-to-numerical coding system, the single letters A-Z are given values of 0-25 respectively. In a three-letter word, the first letter has value α, the second letter has value β, and the third letter has value γ. The value of a three-letter word is computed as follows:

$$\text{word value} = \alpha \cdot 26^2 + \beta \cdot 26^1 + \gamma \cdot 26^0$$

For example:

$$\text{CAT} = 2 \cdot 26^2 + 0 \cdot 26^1 + 19 \cdot 26^0 = 1371$$

What word has the value 783?

(A) ASK

(B) BED

(C) CUP

(D) DOG

(E) ELF

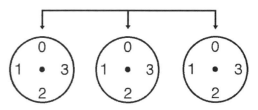

Current Reading: 0 - 0 - 0

10. Each of the three disks shown above rotates clockwise about its center. The disk on the right rotates at the rate of 90° per second. The disk in the middle rotates 90° each time the disk on the right completes one full rotation. The disk on the left rotates 90° each time the disk in the middle completes one full rotation. If the device starts with a reading of 0-0-0, what is its reading after 1 minute has elapsed?

(A) 2-3-0

(B) 2-3-1

(C) 2-3-2

(D) 3-2-2

(E) 3-3-0

End of Section

ETS Dirt XIII

In the late 1970's, the U. S. Federal Trade Commission studied and reported on standardized test coaching. At first, they thought Kaplan and other coaching companies were running scams:

> "In light of the increasing competitiveness for a place in colleges and graduate schools, these representations [that training for the SAT would help] would appeal to all segments of society seeking entrance to institutions of higher learning, and more particularly to graduate schools in the professions. Since these courses sell for $250 and are probably worth closer to $5, almost the entire sales figure for the aptitude courses constitutes consumer injury."[23]

But then, the FTC did a study. Kaplan tells us:

> "The investigation had pitted the College Board against the coaching industry and declared us the winner. The conclusions were daunting. The FTC said that because not all students could afford coaching, the tests created barriers to education opportunities guaranteed by the federal General Education Provisions Act. The report also stated that coaching 'reveals the lack of reliability and validity of these examinations.' "[24]

Today (2010), test prep is a 4 billion dollar industry and ETS offers its very own online prep course for $69.95. According to the College Board: "The official SAT online course is one of the best ways to get ready for the SAT."

Needless to say, CrushTheTest is "unofficial" prep material.

Reading

Charts

median, average, interpretation, careful reading, percents, ratios, costs

Charts

Questions 1-3: The graph below shows the correlation between median SAT math score and family income based on (real) data from FairTest.

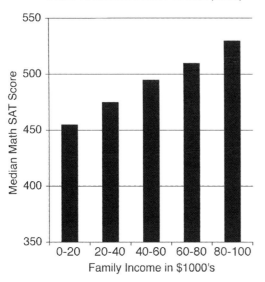

Score vs Income From FairTest (2009)

1. From the lowest scoring income group to the highest scoring income group, the approximate number of points by which the median score increases for each additional $10,000 in family income is:

    (A) 1
    (B) 2
    (C) 10
    (D) 20
    (E) 40

2! Which of the following must be true based on the Score vs. Income graph?

    I. No one whose family earns more than $80,000 scored below 500.

    II. For test-takers whose families earn between $40,000 and $60,000, there were more scores below 475 than above 475.

    III. The median score of all test-takers represented in the chart is closer to 500 than it is to 525.

    (A) none
    (B) I, only
    (C) II, only
    (D) III, only
    (E) II and III, only

3. If the rate of score increase (in points per dollar) between the lowest and second lowest income groups persisted for all income groups, at what income would the median score first reach 800?

    (A) $350,000
    (B) $550,000
    (C) $800,000
    (D) $1,000,000
    (E) $1,250,000

Questions 4-7: Assume that people who use CrushTheTest ("users") and people who do not use CrushTheTest ("non-users") will achieve scores on the math SAT according to the table below. A test score is always a multiple of 10.

scores for 100,000 users and 1,000,000 non-users

score	users (%)	non-users (%)
800	16	1
750-790	40	10
700-740	30	20
600-690	14	30
200-590	0	39

4. The median score for all users could be:

(A) 700

(B) 720

(C) 740

(D) 755

(E) none of these

5. If test-takers scoring in any of the ranges in the table are equally likely to receive any score in the range, what will be the ratio of the number of non-users scoring 720 to the number of users scoring 720?

(A) 2/3

(B) 3/2

(C) 3

(D) 2.5

(E) 6.67

Questions 4-7: Assume that people who use CrushTheTest ("users") and people who do not use CrushTheTest ("non-users") will achieve scores on the math SAT according to the table below. A test score is always a multiple of 10.

scores for 100,000 users and 1,000,000 non-users

score	users (%)	non-users (%)
800	16	1
750-790	40	10
700-740	30	20
600-690	14	30
200-590	0	39

6. If test-takers scoring in any of the ranges in the table are equally likely to receive any score in the range, how many out of a randomly-selected group of 500 non-users would be expected to receive a 650?

(A) 150

(B) 120

(C) 90

(D) 15

(E) 12

7. If users scoring between 750 and 790 are equally likely to receive any score in that range, then, to the nearest point, the average score received by users scoring between 750 and 800 inclusive is:

(A) 761

(B) 766

(C) 769

(D) 775

(E) 779

Questions 8-10: The figure below shows a (fictional) STS budget.

$100,000,000 STS Budget

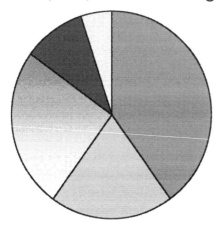

■ Salaries For Big Shots 40%

□ Public Relations 20%

□ Salaries For Ordinary Employees 25%

■ Buildings and Supplies 10%

□ Producing Questions 5%

8. Suppose there are five times as many ordinary employees as big shots. The ratio of the average big shot salary to the average ordinary employee salary is therefore:

(A) 8 to 5

(B) 8 to 1

(C) 5 to 3

(D) 5 to 2

(E) 10 to 1

9. To produce a test question, the STS pays Joe $100 to write five proposed questions and then pays Bob $100 to pick one of the five to be an actual test question. If the average STS test has 100 questions and if questions are not re-used, how many different tests can STS inflict upon us per year?

(A) 1250

(B) 1000

(C) 750

(D) 500

(E) 250

10. In response to criticism of its tests, the STS decides to increase the dollar amount of its public relations (PR) budget by 40% by allocating money from salaries for ordinary employees to PR. What is the new percentage of the budget spent on salaries for ordinary employees?

(A) 17%

(B) 18%

(C) 19%

(D) 20%

(E) 21%

End of Section

ETS Dirt XIV

Bates is another highly selective college in Maine that has made the SAT optional. Bates admits many students who don't submit any test scores. These students, as a group, get the same freshman grades as those who do submit scores, and they actually graduate at a slightly higher rate (almost everyone who goes to Bates ends up graduating).

You can read about Bates and other colleges that have taken the "standardized tests are optional" leap at www.fairtest.org.

The list of SAT optional colleges goes well into the hundreds and includes the following: Antioch, Bates, Bard, Bennington, Bowdoin, Bryn Mawr, Colby, Connecticut College, Hamilton, Hampshire, Lewis and Clark, Middlebury, Mount Holyoke, Pitzer, Sarah Lawrence, University of Texas at Austin, and Wake Forest University.

Keep in mind that at some of these colleges "SAT optional" actually means "if you submit other standardized tests such as Advanced Placement exams, then you don't have to bother with the SAT."

FairTest is a non-profit organization that is not particularly fond of the SAT.

Logic

Reasoning

multiple if-then statements, quadratics, number characteristics, long word problems, information sufficiency, define and use new symbol

Reasoning

1. Bob and Carol and Ted and Alice either hate or love each of the other three people. The following is true:

Bob loves Ted and hates Carol
Carol loves two of the other three people
Carol hates everyone who hates her
Only one person loves Alice

Therefore, which must be true:

I.   Ted hates Alice

II.   Ted loves Carol

III. Ted loves Bob

(A) none

(B) I, only

(C) II, only

(D) I and II, only

(E) II and III only

2. Bob and Carol and Ted and Alice smuggle treasure from a Caribbean island to the United States. The FBI is onto them. There are four possible outcomes and each of our four heroes will experience one outcome and each will experience a different outcome.

Bob or Carol or Ted will go to jail.
Ted or Alice will get rich.
Carol or Alice will change her identity.
Bob or Ted or Alice will go into hiding.

Which of the following is true?

I.   If Bob goes to jail, Alice gets rich.

II.   If Ted goes to jail, Bob goes into hiding.

III. If Carol goes to jail, Ted gets rich.

(A) III, only

(B) I and II, only

(C) I and III, only

(D) II and III, only

(E) I, II, and III

3. If the equation below is true for all values of x and if $b > 0$, then what is the value of b?

$$x^2 + 3bx + b + c = (x+b)(x+c)$$

(A) 0.5

(B) 1

(C) 1.5

(D) 2

(E) 2.5

4. If $ax^2 + bx + c = 0$ for all values of x then which of the following is true?

I. $a = b = c = 0$

II. $a > b + c$

III. $a^2 > b^2 + c^2$

(A) none

(B) I, only

(C) II, only

(D) III, only

(E) II and III, only

5! If n is an integer, for how many values of n does $x^2 + nx + n = 0$ have integer solutions?

(A) none

(B) one

(C) two

(D) three

(E) more than three

6. If $ab = cd$ and $a > b > c > d$ then which of the following must be true?

I. $a > 0$

II. $|b| = |c|$

III. $|c| < |d|$

(A) I, only

(B) II, only

(C) I and II, only

(D) I and III, only

(E) II and III, only

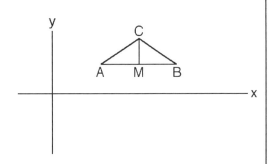

7. If line segment AB is parallel to the *x*-axis and M is the midpoint of AB and CM is perpendicular to AB, which of the following is sufficient additional information, by itself, to determine the area of triangle ABC?

I. the *xy* coordinates of A and C

II. the *xy* coordinates of A and B

III. the *xy* coordinates of C and M

(A) none

(B) I, only

(C) III, only

(D) I and III, only ✓

(E) I, II, and III ✗

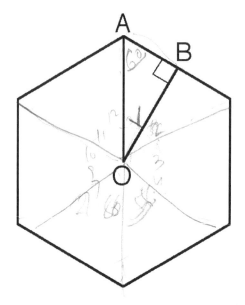

8. Which of the following statements would, if true, provide sufficient additional information to determine the perimeter of the regular hexagon with center O shown in the figure?

I. ✓The length of AO is 2 inches.

II. ✓ The length of BO is 2 inches.

III. ✓ The perimeter of ΔAOB is 2 inches.

(A) I, only

(B) II, only

(C) I or II, only

(D) I or III, only

(E) I or II or III ✓

9. A positive number x has three digits and $\sim x$ is defined as the number obtained by adding 1 to each digit that is less than 9 while leaving 9's unchanged. Which of the following must be true?

I. $\sim(\sim x) > \sim x$

II. $\sim x \geq x + 100$

III. $3x > \sim x$

(A) none

(B) I, only

(C) II, only

(D) III, only

(E) I, II, and III

10. For a number n $(n \neq 0)$,
$$\ddagger n = \frac{1}{n}$$
and
$$*n = 1 - \frac{1}{n}.$$
Therefore, for a number m $(m \neq 0,1)$,
$$*(\ddagger(*m)) -$$

(A) m

(B) $\ddagger m$

(C) $*m$

(D) $\ddagger(\ddagger m)$

(E) $*(*m)$

End of Section

ETS Dirt XV

Here's a fun question taken from an ETS Achievement Test in chemistry given in the 1960's and reproduced in Owen's book.[25] Noted physicist and Einstein collaborator Banesh Hoffmann pointed out to ETS that the question had no answer. Then, as now, ETS was a model of stubbornness — a veritable guru to stubborn people everywhere.[26]

> The burning of gasoline in an automobile cylinder involves all of the following *except*:
>
> A) reduction
>
> B) decomposition
>
> C) an exothermic reaction
>
> D) oxidation
>
> E) conversion of matter to energy

Hoffmann explained to ETS that the most famous equation in science, $E = mc^2$, means that ALL releases of energy are accompanied by a change in mass. ETS replied that since the change in mass is extremely small [due to the large value of c in Einstein's equation] it therefore doesn't count.[27]

Not the tightest reasoning in the world but apparently preferable to admitting a mistake. For the full ETS argument see note #27 in the References and Notes section.

ETS probably still thinks (E) is the answer and, let's face it, you *should* pick (E) and move on to the next question. Keep the historic weakness of ETS exams in the back of your mind while choosing the answers *they* will mark correct.

Dr. Banesh "there is no correct answer" Hoffmann (1906-1986) wrote the classic *Albert Einstein Creator and Rebel* and *The Tyranny of Testing* among other books and articles.

Counting

Combinations

distribution of objects, creation of teams, combinations, combinations with exceptions, number of routes

Sequences

sum of numbers in a sequence, determination of nth number in a sequence, complex rules for determining members of a sequence

Combinations

1. Positive integer N is the product of four different prime numbers w, x, y, and z. How many different factors does N have (including itself and 1)?

(A) 6

(B) 12

(C) 16

(D) 20

(E) cannot be determined

2! Bob and Carol and Ted and Alice see 3 silver dollars lying on the street. They run for the money and a fight ensues. At the end of the battle, all three silver dollars are spoken for. One possible outcome is Bob has 2 of the silver dollars, Carol has 1, and Ted and Alice have none. How many such possible outcomes are there?

(A) 12

(B) 20

(C) 24

(D) 64

(E) 81

3. One four-person team will be created from 4 boys and 4 girls. If the team must have two boys and two girls, how many different possible teams might be created?

(A) 16

(B) 32

(C) 36

(D) 64

(E) 144

4. Alice, Bob, Carol, David, and Ted are going to sit down in five chairs. The chairs are numbered 1-5. Ted is superstitious and will not sit in chair #3 as he notes that SAT has three letters and has concluded, possibly erroneously, that 3 is an unlucky number. The chairs are not moved, each person chooses one chair, and Ted does not choose chair #3. In how many different ways may the five people arrange themselves among the five chairs?

(A) 60

(B) 75

(C) 90

(D) 96

(E) 105

5. A group of T people were surveyed about the SAT and asked to check <u>one or two</u> of the choices below.

What is your opinion of the SAT?
$\bigcirc$ it is evil
$\bigcirc$ it sucks

In each of the T surveys, at least one oval was checked. A total of x "it is evil" checks were counted and a total of y "it sucks" checks were counted. The positive integer B is the number of surveys in which <u>both</u> choices were checked.

Which of the following statements must be true?

I. $x + y = T + B$

II. The number of people who checked only "it is evil" is $x - B$.

III. If $x = B$, everyone checked "it is evil."

(A) II, only

(B) III, only

(C) I and II, only

(D) II and III only

(E) I, II, and III

6. N points are placed on line segment AB so that, including points A and B, there are $N+2$ points on AB. The additional points are labeled A_1, A_2, A_3, *etc.*, and all possible line segments with labeled endpoints are considered (AA_1, AA_2, A_2A_3, A_2B, *etc.*). How many <u>different</u> line segments are there?

(A) $N^2 + N + 1$

(B) $N^2 + 3N + 1$

(C) $N^2 + 3N + 2$

(D) $\frac{1}{2}N^2 + 3N + 2$

(E) $\frac{1}{2}N^2 + \frac{3}{2}N + 1$

7. To gain an advantage on the SAT, some students study CrushTheTest (CTT), some study previous unpublished tests obtained from friends, some study both CTT and previous tests, and some poor saps do neither. If 25% of students do neither and if the number of students who study both CTT and previous tests is half the number who study only CTT and one-third the number who study only previous tests, then what percentage of students study only CTT?

(A) 5

(B) 10

(C) 15

(D) 20

(E) 25

8. From the secret headquarters of the fictional Standardized Testing Service (STS), three underground roads each lead directly to the big boss's office. From SATAN's office, three more roads each wind ever deeper to the Eternal Testing Center (ETC) where bad people spend all eternity taking and re-taking the SAT. How many different routes are there from STS to the ETC and back if no route can use the same road twice?

(A) 9

(B) 18

(C) 27

(D) 36

(E) 45

9. A teacher at the TSA (Testing School of America) finally gets fed up with giving tests. So she makes a deal with her twenty-student class: there will be no tests. At the end of the year, students will pick their grade out of a hat which will contain 20 slips of paper each with a different integer between 81 and 100 inclusive written on it. The piece of paper you pick will be your grade for the year. Pieces of paper will NOT be returned to the hat after they are picked. You have a friend in the class whose name is Joe. What is the probability that you and Joe will be within one point of each other after you have each picked a grade?

(A) 1/10

(B) 1/19

(C) 1/20

(D) 1/21

(E) 1/30

10. If a, b, and c are positive integers, how many ordered triplets (a, b, c) satisfy the equation below?

$$a^3 \cdot b^2 \cdot c = 64$$

(A) 3

(B) 4

(C) 5

(D) 6

(E) 7

End of Section

ETS Dirt XVI

Here's a question: What's the hardest part of a (insert the name of your favorite big name school) education? If you said "getting in," you're right.

If you want to get in to a name school, you should know what you're dealing with — read *The Price of Admission* by Daniel Golden.[28] It's a well-documented, fairly opinionated, hard-hitting look at how top college admissions actually work.

Legacies, athletes, celebrities and their children, under-represented minorities, faculty children, big donors, politically-connected families, and students attending elite private and public high schools have a surprisingly big edge. In the parlance of your friendly neighborhood admissions officer, everyone else is "unhooked."[29] They get to compete with students who have "juice."[30]

It is reasonable for top colleges to seek talented athletes, ethnic diversity, and even billionaire heirs — they are, after all, private institutions. However, admissions preferences have a big effect and should not be ignored. According to one estimate, *more than half* of all students accepted at big name schools get in due to a nonacademic preference.[31]

Here are some rules of thumb we put together based on statistics[32] provided by Golden in *The Price of Admission*. First, if you are unhooked, you have to cut the acceptance rate of the school in half in order to properly evaluate your chances. So if the school accepts 20% of *all* applicants, they will accept roughly 10% of *unhooked* applicants. Second, you'll need *at least* 50 points above the school's median *on each section* of the SAT just to be competitive.

It is not always thus. Caltech, for example, doesn't do juice.[33] They are the exception among top schools. You'll still need near-perfect SAT's, however, along with evidence of real academic talent.

Sequences

1. What is the last digit in 7^{503}?

   (A) 1

   (B) 3

   (C) 5

   (D) 7

   (E) 9

2. The fraction 1/7 is equal to 0.142857142857 . . . The first digit after the decimal point is 1. What is the sum of the first 100 digits after the decimal point?

   (A) 432

   (B) 435

   (C) 440

   (D) 445

   (E) 447

3. In the sequence 1, 2, 3, 1, 2, 3 . . . the first digit is a 1, the second digit is a 2, the third digit is a 3, the fourth digit is a 1 *etc*. A subset S of this sequence consists of every 10th digit starting with the 10th digit, the 20th digit, and the 30th digit, up to and including the 1000th digit. There are 100 digits in subset S. What is the sum of the digits in subset S?

(A) 190

(B) 191

(C) 199

(D) 209

(E) 210

$$x, \ldots, a$$

4. In the sequence shown above, the first term is x and the 6th term is a. If each term in the sequence after the first is obtained by dividing the previous term by 2 and then squaring the result, which of the expressions below gives the value of x in terms of the value of a?

(A) $2^{\frac{63}{32}} \cdot a^{\frac{1}{64}}$

(B) $2^{\frac{31}{16}} \cdot a^{\frac{1}{32}}$

(C) $2^{\frac{31}{16}} \cdot a^{\frac{1}{64}}$

(D) $2^{\frac{63}{32}} \cdot a^{\frac{1}{32}}$

(E) $2^{\frac{1}{64}} \cdot a^{\frac{31}{16}}$

154

$a, \ldots$

5. In the sequence above, the terms are numbered by the positive integer n. The first term in the sequence ($n = 1$) is a. Terms of the sequence after the first that have odd values of n are obtained by dividing the previous term by 2. Terms of the sequence that have even values of n are obtained by multiplying the previous term by 10. What is the 89th term in the sequence?

(A) $5^{44} \cdot a$

(B) $5^{45} \cdot a$

(C) $2 \cdot 5^{44} \cdot a$

(D) $2 \cdot 5^{45} \cdot a$

(E) $10 \cdot 5^{45} \cdot a$

$a, b, \ldots$

6. In the sequence above, the first term is positive integer a and the second term is positive integer b. Each term after the second term is equal to the sum of the two immediately preceding terms. The ratio of the 8th term in the sequence to the third term in the sequence is 11. Which of the following could be the value of the product ab?

(A) 20

(B) 30

(C) 36

(D) 48

(E) 54

7. A sequence of integers is numbered from 1 to n where n is the position of the integer in the sequence. The nth term of the sequence ($n>1$) is obtained by multiplying the value of the previous term by -1 and then taking the result to the power of -n. Thus, if the first term is a, the second term is $(-a)^{-2}$. If the second term is b, the third term is $(-b)^{-3}$. If the value of the first term in the sequence is 1, what is the value of the sum of the first ten terms in the sequence?

(A) -8

(B) -2

(C) 0

(D) 2

(E) 8

A	B	C	D	E	F	G	H
0	1/6	1/3	1/2	2/3	3/4	5/6	1

8. On the number line shown above, the length of line segment AH is 1 and the distances of points B, C, D, E, F, and G from point A have the fractional values shown. If all possible pairs of different labeled points are considered and if the length of each line segment, including AH, is calculated, how many different lengths will be obtained?

(A) 7

(B) 8

(C) 9

(D) 10

(E) 11

9. Four consecutive, positive, even integers a, b, c, and d will be chosen such that $0<a<b<c<d$. If the sum, S, of the four integers must be less than 500, which of the following is the number of possible values of S?

(A) 56

(B) 60

(C) 120

(D) 125

(E) 499

$a, b, c, a, a, b, b, c, c, a, a, a, ...$

10. In a sequence containing the letters a, b, and c, shown above, the number of repetitions of a given letter increases by 1 each time the letter reappears. In the first 90 terms of this sequence, how many times does the letter b appear?

(A) 28

(B) 30

(C) 32

(D) 34

(E) 36

End of Section

ETS Dirt XVII

In *None of the Above*, David Owen unleashes a well-constructed attack on the quality of the SAT (especially the verbal section), on its validity, and on the fairness of having so much ride on the test.

Stanley Kaplan, on the other hand, thinks highly of the SAT and of testing in general as opportunities for people to prove themselves. In *Test Pilot* he tells the story of a brilliant and promising 16-year-old high school graduate who was admitted to Columbia in the 1930's but couldn't go because his family didn't have the money. Even though he graduated second in his class from City College in New York, he was rejected by five out of five medical schools! In those days, graduating from a public college and having a Jewish last name were a deadly combination.[34]

Today, we have the MCAT — the Medical College Admission Test. A 21st century Stanley Kaplan would not get five rejection letters.

So what does the math SAT mean for a top student?

First of all, the hard questions on the math part of the SAT are good, clever questions. Second, building up your superficial math ability — speed, accuracy, and cleverness — isn't an entirely unreasonable use of time. Third, preparing for the SAT and trying to get a high score can be fun if you like math and puzzles.

Training for the SAT can make the difference between a good score and a killer score. The killer score does <u>not</u> mean you are any better-prepared for college. However, since most colleges still overestimate the value of high SAT scores (the SAT is an irresistible shortcut for them), it makes sense to go for the 800.

And why shouldn't you get an 800 (or close to it) anyway? Sure, long term, it's more or less meaningless. But so what? Take the money and run.

Answers

DON'T LOOK!

The answers are on the back of this page. Cut them out and give them to your assistant. Tell your assistant not to tell you the answers no matter what. They are only allowed to tell you whether or not you got 10 out of 10 on a section.

Only this and nothing more.

See page 2 for details about the CrushTheTest 10-out-of-10-or-nothing Training Technique.

DON'T COMPROMISE!

Algebra: Warmup	CBDCDDEEAE
Algebra: Manipulation	CACEECDADC
Algebra: Fractions	BAEBEDBCCB
Algebra: Functions	ACAABEAEDB
Algebra: Word Problems	DEAECCBEAB
Geometry: Lengths, Angles, . . .	BDABCEDADE
Geometry: Areas	AECDDBBDBE
Geometry: Triangles	BEDEAEEDAD
Geometry: Points and Space	CBCCEEDDCA
Units: Prices, Percents, 2D, 3D	BECDDACCAE
Units: Algebra	ACCBACBABB
Statistics: Warmup	CBBEABEDCE
Statistics: Averages	AADDDEBBDB
Statistics: Probability	ABADBDDEBD
Statistics: Mean, Median, Mode	ACCEAADABA
Numbers: Divisibility	BEEBABCDDC
Numbers: Characteristics	DCDDACAADB
Numbers: Remainders	DCCAEDACDA
Numbers: Digitology	ADBCBEDEBE
Reading: Charts	CAADEDEBEA
Logic: Reasoning	DDCBCDBEDB
Counting: Combinations	CBCDCEEDAE
Counting: Sequences	BECBAEDEBA

Notes and References

1. *The Official SAT Study Guide,* Educational Testing Service (2008).

2. Owen, David *None of the Above: The Truth Behind the SATs*, Rowan and Littlefield Publishers Inc., Revised Updated Edition (1999) 0-8476-9507-7.

3. Owen, p. 54.

4. Owen, p. 128. Here's the full quote: "ETS claims, somewhat incredibly, that the SAT is 'relatively unspeeded' based on the fact that virtually everyone 'finishes' at least three quarters of the exam. But a student who answered the last question and no other would be said to have 'finished' the test. Although it is true that low-scoring students often find themselves with time on their hands when they take the SAT, because they don't even attempt the harder questions, higher-scoring students know that test-taking speed can make an enormous difference."

5. Owen, p. 43.

6. Owen, p. 46.

7. Owen, pp. 61-63.

8. Owen, p. 63.

9. Owen, p. 133.

10. Owen, p. 238.

11. Owen, p. 86.

12. Owen, p. 87.

13. Owen, p. 98.

14. Owen, p. 100.

15. Owen, pp. 100-101.

16. Kaplan, Stanley *Test Pilot,* Simon and Schuster (2001) 0-7432-0168-X, p. 68.

17. Kaplan, p. 111.

18. Owen, p. 131.

19. Kaplan, p. 96.

20. Kaplan, p. 66.

21. Kaplan, p. 66.

22. Kaplan, pp. 26, 34, 48.

23. Kaplan, pp. 91-92.

24. Kaplan, p. 108.

25. Owen, p. 54.

26. Owen, p. 55.

27. Owen, p. 55. Here's the full ETS argument with [CrushTheTest comments]: "The superior student is as aware of the *classical* concepts of matter and chemical change as he is aware of the model of *modern* physics. He is likely to be more aware than is the average student that the 'conversion of matter into energy' has been demonstrated only for nuclear changes [as far as we know, $E = mc^2$ is *always* true]. Perhaps he realizes that if [???] the energy freed by the burning gasoline comes from the conversion of mass into energy [as 100% of it does], the loss in mass is only about a ten-billionth of the mass of the gasoline burned, a loss too small to be measured by available methods."

28. Golden, Daniel *The Price of Admission* Three Rivers Press, New York (2006) 978-1-4000-9797-5.

29. Golden, p. 14.

30. Golden, p. 184.

31. Golden, pp. 6-7.

32. Golden, pp. 4, 5, 19, 89, 180, 203.

33. Golden, pp. 261-264, 277-284.

34. Kaplan, pp. 23-25.

Book II: Solutions

Book II mirrors the main book.

All questions are repeated with answer choices replaced by solutions.

To find the solution to a problem on page 50 of Book I, go to page A50 in Book II.

Suggestion: Don't go to the solution right away. Struggle with each problem you get wrong. Do battle. That way, when a similar problem appears on the real SAT, you'll be ready.

Table of Contents: Book II

Algebra

Warmup

basics, easy, not SAT-like

Manipulation

words-to-equations, rearranging equations, exponents including fractional and negative exponents, square roots, cube roots

Fractions

ratios, proportions, compounding, algebra problems using fractions

Functions

$f(x)$ language, matching graph to $f(x)$, shifting graphs up/down and left/right, intersection points, algebra problems using functions

Word Problems

compounding costs, speed-distance-time problems, words-to-equations-to-solutions, given constraints produce equation or possible answer

Warmup

1. If $x = \dfrac{1}{p}$ then $\dfrac{1}{x} =$

Just turn it upside down. The answer is p (C).

---

2. If $w = x^a$ and $z = x^b$ then $wz =$

Add the exponents.

Think of it this way: $x^2 = x \cdot x$ and $x^3 = x \cdot x \cdot x$ so $x^2 \cdot x^3 = x \cdot x \cdot x \cdot x \cdot x = x^5$.

In the same way $\left(x^2\right)^3 = x^2 \cdot x^2 \cdot x^2$ which x^6.

When you multiply you add the two exponents. When you raise to a power, you multiply the two exponents.

The answer is x^{a+b} (B).

3. The quantity $(ab)^{-5} =$

The negative sign means "1 over." So,

$$(ab)^{-5} = \frac{1}{(ab) \cdot (ab) \cdot (ab) \cdot (ab) \cdot (ab)} = \frac{1}{a^5 b^5}.$$

When in doubt, write it out. The answer is (D).

---

4. The quantity $\dfrac{xy^2 + y}{y} =$

For every y you cancel on the bottom you must cancel a y in BOTH terms on top.

When something cancels completely, it doesn't vanish – it leaves a 1 behind. So,

$$\frac{xy^2 + y}{y} = xy + 1.$$

The answer is (C).

<u>Note</u>: If one of the terms on top runs out of y's, you're done canceling. So,

$$\frac{xy^8 + y^2}{y^3} = \frac{xy^6 + 1}{y}.$$

Sometimes you can't do much of anything. So,

$$\frac{xy^5 + 1}{y^2} = \frac{xy^5 + 1}{y^2}.$$

5. The quantity $\dfrac{x-1}{1-x} =$

When you switch two things you're subtracting, you get a negative sign. For example: $2-3 = -(3-2)$.

So the answer is –1 (D).

---

6. The quantity $x^2 - y^2 =$

Difference of squares, cross term cancels, blah, blah, blah.

Of course the answer is $(x+y)(x-y)$ or (D).

7. If $\dfrac{a}{b} = \dfrac{x}{y}$ and $x \neq 0$ then

The real SAT doesn't have "all of these" as an answer unless they use their I, II, III format and say "which of the following must be true?"

You do want to have your proportions down, however. You can turn both sides upside down, switch x and b, switch a and y, multiply both sides by y, or multiply both sides by b.

The answer is "all of these" or (E).

---

8. If k is a positive number then k percent of x is equal to:

Always convert a percent to a decimal or fraction so you have something you can calculate with. For example:

"30 percent of" means multiply by 0.3.

"k percent of" means multiply by $k/100$.

For this question, the answer is $kx/100$ or (E).

Another example:

If n people use CrushTheTest out of N people who take the SAT, the fraction of people with a huge advantage is n/N.

The percent of people with a huge advantage is $100n/N$.

9. If y is the result of increasing x by 30 percent then $y =$

The new, good, fast one-step method:

Increasing by 30% means multiply by 1.3.

Decreasing by 30% means multiply by 0.7.

The old, bad, clunky two-step method:

To increase by 30%, multiply by 0.3 and then add it to whatever you started with. To decrease by 30%, multiply by 0.3 and subtract.

Use the one-step method.

The answer is $1.3x$ or (A).

10. The square root of x cubed is equal to:

$$\sqrt{x^3} = \sqrt{x^2 \cdot x} = \sqrt{x^2}\sqrt{x} = x\sqrt{x}.$$

So the answer is (E).

<u>Note</u>: It is a common mistake to forget that

$$\sqrt{x+y} \neq \sqrt{x} + \sqrt{y}$$

and

$$\sqrt{x^2 + y^2} \neq x + y.$$

End of Section

Basic Algebra Tips

<u>When a house-elf makes a mistake he bangs his head against the wall.</u>

Write stuff down.

Write neatly.

Minimize calculator use.

Check your work (quickly) before moving on.

Did you answer the question they asked?

Did you miss any factors of two?

Did you miss any negative signs?

Are you a prim and proper stiff and starched bookkeeper or a filthy good-for-nothing smelly stinking slob?

SATAN favors bookkeepers.

(You can go back to being a slob after the test!)

Manipulation

1. Jason rents out his family's house while they are on vacation. He charges y dollars per day for the rental and receives a 20 dollar tip from the renters. Jason's family has five members including Jason, and all of the money Jason receives from the renters including the tip is divided evenly amongst the five family members. Jason spends 6 dollars of his share leaving him with z dollars from the rental venture. Which of the following represents number of days the house was occupied by the renters?

They are asking you for the number of days the house was occupied but there is no variable for this mentioned in the problem. This makes the problem hard inasmuch as it will "get" many students.

You have to define your own variable, say n, for the number of days and then convert the words into an equation.

Start with ny for the amount he charges then get $ny + 20$ to include the tip. Then divide by 5 because he his splitting it with his family. You get: $(ny + 20) / 5$.

Now subtract 6 and set equal to z to get:

$$z = \frac{ny+20}{5} - 6 \implies n = \frac{5z+10}{y} \ .$$

So the answer is (C).

2. If $9^{b+1} = a^8$ then $27^b =$

The SAT doesn't test logs and all problems can be done without a calculator.

First switch everything to the same base:

$$9^{b+1} = 3^{2(b+1)} \text{ and } 27^b = 3^{3b}.$$

So we have $3^{2(b+1)} = a^8$ and we need 3^{3b}. If we square root both sides we get $3^{(b+1)} = a^4$. Then we get the constant out of the exponent like so:

$$3^{(b+1)} = 3^1 \cdot 3^b = a^4 \implies 3^b = \frac{a^4}{3}.$$

Now all you have to do is cube both sides and you're done!

Or, you might take a somewhat longer route:

$$3^{2(b+1)} = 3^{2b+2} = 3^{2b} \cdot 3^2 = 9 \cdot 3^{2b} = a^8 \implies 3^{2b} = \frac{a^8}{9}.$$

Unfortunately, we're not there yet. We still have to turn a $2b$ in an exponent into a $3b$. We raise it to the 3/2 power like so:

$$27^b = 3^{3b} = (3^{2b})^{3/2} = \left(\frac{a^8}{9}\right)^{3/2} = \frac{a^{12}}{27}.$$

The answer is (A).

<u>Note</u>: Of course, $9^{3/2}$ is another way of saying "the square root of 9 cubed" which is 27. It's easier to do the square root first and then cube the result.

3. If $x = 2b$ and $a = 3$ then $\dfrac{2^{a-b}}{2^x} =$

Checking the answers, you see there's no a or x so you start by substituting to get $2^{3-b}/2^{2b}$.

Now use the rules for exponents (dividing means subtracting) to get $2^{3-b-2b} = 2^{3-3b}$.

You see some 8's in the answers and you know of course that SATAN loves the fact that $2^3 = 8$.

So you factor your exponent a bit to get $2^{3-3b} = 2^{3(1-b)}$.

Now you have:

$2^{3(1-b)} = \left(2^3\right)^{(1-b)} = 8^{1-b}$.

So the answer is (C).

<u>Note</u>: This is an especially nasty application of the rule: $x^{ab} = (x^a)^b$.

4. If $r + s + t = r - u = s - t$ then which of the following is true?

I. $r = -2t$

II. $s + t + u = 0$

III. $r + 2s = 2(s - t)$

To check I, you need to solve for r in terms of t. If you set the first expression equal to the third expression you get $r+s+t=s-t$ and you can verify I by getting r by itself.

For II, you need to find $s+t+u$. You'll get what you want by adding u to both sides of the first and second expressions and canceling the r's. So II is true.

You can get III directly from the given by adding an s to both sides of the first and third expressions and then subtracting t from both sides and then factoring out a 2 on the right side.

But suppose you don't see that and you are feeling confused by III. If that happens, SWITCH GEARS, and try working backwards starting with III and seeing what you get.

Suddenly you see that the two $2s$ terms in III cancel and you are back to I which you already know is true.

So the answer is (E).

5. If $x = \dfrac{ab+c}{a}$ then $xb =$

SATAN loves questions that look strange. But they can't be testing you on anything other than ordinary algebra. When you look at this one, you soon realize that you can't manipulate it to get xb so you STOP.

You look at the answers. They have everything in them but b. You stare at the problem for 10 seconds and take a breath. You remind yourself it has to be easy. If you don't see what do to at this point you MOVE ON (you can always come back).

If you do see their little trick, you realize the only way to not have b in the answer is to solve for b.

Whew! SATAN is held a bay once again by our hero. You get $b = (ax - c)/a$, multiply by x, and you're done! Here it is:

$$bx = \frac{ax - c}{a} \cdot \frac{x}{1} = \frac{ax^2 - cx}{a}.$$

The answer is (E).

6. If $x^{\frac{8}{3}} = y^{\frac{6}{7}}$ and $y > 0$ then $x^2 \cdot y^{-\frac{3}{7}} =$

They don't test logarithms on the SAT so there has to be some easier way.

Look for something simple, like a relationship between $y^{(3/7)}$ and $y^{(6/7)}$.

It has to be easy and it is easy — one is the square root of the other. Taking a square root is the same as multiplying the exponent by $1/2$.

SATAN would never say "take the square root of $x^{(8/3)}$" because that would be too obvious.

So now we have $y^{(3/7)} = x^{(4/3)}$ which means $y^{-(3/7)} = x^{-(4/3)}$. Substitute and multiply:

$$x^2 \cdot x^{-4/3} = x^{6/3} \cdot x^{-4/3} = x^{2/3} = \sqrt[3]{x^2}.$$

The answer is (C).

Here it is from the beginning:

$$x^2 \cdot y^{-3/7} = x^2 \cdot \sqrt{y^{-6/7}} = x^2 \cdot \sqrt{x^{-8/3}} = x^2 \cdot x^{-4/3} = x^{2/3}.$$

Since March 2005, they've been getting more vicious with the fractional and negative exponents but the problems always look harder than they really are.

7! If $a^2 = b^2 = c^2 = d^2$ then the average of a, b, c, and d expressed in terms of a could be:

There are <u>four</u> possible averages. The key is to realize that the four numbers don't have to have the same sign. Textbook problems don't usually have multiple possibilities like this; that's why SATAN likes this kind of problem.

The most obvious possible average is just a. This would be the case if $a = b = c = d$. They could all be –4 for example or they could all be some positive number like +6. Either way, the average would be a.

The next most obvious possible average is zero. This would happen if your four numbers were evenly split between positive and negative: *e.g.*, (4, 4, –4, –4).

On the other hand, suppose $a = b = c$ but d was the negative of the other three (*e.g.*, 4, 4, 4, –4). Then c and d would cancel out of the sum and the average would be $(a+b)/4 = 2a/4 = a/2$.

Finally, you could have $b = c = d$ with a the negative of the other three (*e.g.*, 4, –4, –4, –4). Then you'd get

$$\frac{a+b+c+d}{4} = \frac{c+d}{4} = \frac{2c}{4} = \frac{c}{2} = -\frac{a}{2}$$

for the average. This is the least obvious possibility so it is the answer (D).

8. If $x + y \neq 0$, for what values of x is the equation below true?
$$2^{|-x-y|} = \frac{1}{2^{-x-y}}$$

The first step is to use the fact that $1/2^{-a} = 2^a$ to simplify the right side of the equation. We get:

$$2^{|-x-y|} = 2^{x+y}.$$

Next, we can use the fact that $-x-y = -(x+y)$ to simplify the left side of the equation. We get:

$$2^{|-(x+y)|} = 2^{x+y}.$$

You might be tempted to think the equation above is always true. But what if $x+y$ is negative? Then $-(x+y)$ would be positive and the correct equation would be $2^{|-(x+y)|} = 2^{-(x+y)}$.

The equation given in the problem is only true if $x+y$ is positive:

$$x + y > 0 \implies x > -y.$$

The answer is (A).

<u>Note 1</u>: Absolute value signs have some odd behavior: $|-x| = x$ if $x > 0$ and $|-x| = -x$ if $x < 0$. Also, $|x| = x$ if $x > 0$ and $|x| = -x$ if $x < 0$. Remember, $-x$ isn't necessarily negative.

<u>Note 2</u>: The only other way for the equation in the problem to be true is if $x + y = 0$ so you'd get $1 = 1$ from the equation. The problem statement excluded this possibility.

9. If $y + 2^{x+2} = 2^{x+3}$ then which of the following expresses $2^{\frac{x+2}{2}}$ in terms of y?

First, rewrite the equation without those nasty summed exponents:

$$y + 2^2 \cdot 2^x = 2^3 \cdot 2^x$$

Next, solve for y and get 2^x by itself:

$$y = 4 \cdot 2^x \implies \frac{y}{4} = 2^x$$

Now we have to simplify $2^{(x+2)/2}$:

$$2^{(x+2)/2} = \sqrt{2^{x+2}} = \sqrt{2^2 \cdot 2^x} = \sqrt{4 \cdot 2^x}.$$

Therefore:

$$2^{\frac{x+2}{2}} = \sqrt{4 \cdot 2^x} = \sqrt{y}.$$

So the answer is (D).

10. If $\dfrac{x+y}{x-y} = a$ and a, x, and y are positive numbers greater than 1 and $y \neq x$ then $y =$

Multiply by $(x-y)$ to get rid of the fraction and get:

$$x + y = ax - ay.$$

Now you need to group the x's and y's so you can factor out a y and get $y = whatever$.

Add ay to both sides, subtract x from both sides, and get:

$$y(a+1) = x(a-1).$$

Divide both sides by $(a+1)$ to get

$$y = \frac{x(a-1)}{a+1}.$$

You still don't have any of the answers but if you distribute the x in the numerator you get (C).

<u>Note</u>: Trying this one in your head could be fatal.

End of Section

Manipulation Tips

The story of SATAN and his torrid love affair with $2^3 = 8$.

Convert words to equations mechanically. Don't think too much.

Look at the answer choices first. What variables must be eliminated?

Negative exponents: it's a fraction.

Fractional exponents: the bottom is a root, the top is a power.

Multiplying a power by 1/2 is the same as taking the square root.

$$x^2 = x^{6/3} = 1/x^{-6/3}$$

$$2^{x+1} = 2 \cdot 2^x$$

$$2^{x+1} + 2^x = 3 \cdot 2^x$$

$$(2^{2x})^{3/2} = 2^{3x} = 8^x$$

Stay flexible. If one method doesn't work, switch gears.

Watch for SATAN's cancellation trick: "There's a $2s$ on both sides!"

If there are a few possibilities just work them all out.

If it looks funny or impossible, stop and stare.

Powers of 2: 2, 4, 8, 16, 32, 64, 128, 256, 512, 1024

Powers of 3: 3, 9, 27, 81, 243, 729

Powers of 4: 4, 16, 64, 256, 1024

Powers of 5: 5, 25, 125, 625

Powers of 6: 6, 36, 216

Fractions

1. If you pour half of a full small bucket of water into an empty big bucket, the big bucket will be three-tenths full. How many times bigger than the small bucket is the big bucket?

Q. In math language, what are they asking?

A. They are asking: What is $b/s = $ big/small?

(This is a translation of the second English sentence and we're simultaneously defining variables.)

Now we have to translate the first English sentence. It says:

$$\frac{1}{2}s = \frac{3}{10}b.$$

Multiply both sides by $(10/3)$ and divide by s to get:

$$\frac{b}{s} = \frac{5}{3} = 1\frac{2}{3} = 1.67.$$

The answer is (B).

<u>Note</u>: Usually it's one sentence for one equation.

2. A small bucket holds 80 percent of the volume of a big bucket. The big bucket is two-thirds full with water. The small bucket is empty. What fraction of the small bucket do you need to fill with water to have just enough liquid to finish filling the big bucket?

The first sentence translates as:

$$s = \frac{4}{5}b.$$

We translate the third "What fraction of . . . " sentence like so:

$$x \cdot s = \frac{1}{3}b$$

where x is the unknown "fraction of the small bucket" and the $1/3$ comes from the fact that the big bucket is already $2/3$ full.

Can we get x? We'd better be able to at this point. On the SAT once you write your equations, the answer has to be right there. Remember, they can't ask anything really hard.

To get x, we need $1/3$ of b/s and we get b/s from the first equation and substitute:

$$x = \frac{1}{3} \cdot \frac{b}{s} = \frac{1}{3} \cdot \frac{5}{4} = \frac{5}{12}.$$

The answer is (A).

3. Rectangle ACDE is twice as long as it is wide. Point B is one-quarter of the way between points A and C. One ant crawls from point B through point A to point E along the edge of the rectangle traveling a total distance of 10 cm. Another ant crawls from point B through points C and D to point E along the edge of the rectangle traveling a total distance of x cm. How far does the second ant travel?

Let's use s for the smallest distance in the problem, in this case, AB. This way we'll use all whole numbers and only have fractions at the end.

Point B is a quarter way up so we get AC = $4s$ and BC = $3s$.

Since the length is double the width, CD = $8s$ and AE = $8s$. Of course DE = $4s$.

The first ant crawls a distance $s+8s=9s=10$ cm. This means $s = 10/9$.

The second ant crawls $3s+8s+4s=15s$. Plug in s to get $150/9 = 50/3 = 16.67$ cm (E).

4. Line segments AC, BC, CD, CE, and BD are shown above. The length of BC is equal to p percent of the length of AC. The length of CD is equal to p percent of the length of CE. If the length of BD is half the length of AC and one-third the length of CE, then what is the value of p?

This is a classic "parts add up to the whole" problem. First translate:

$BC = p \cdot AC$ and $CD = p \cdot CE$.

Technically, p is a fraction in the equation above; we'll turn it into a percent at the end.

We were also told:

$BD = BC + CD = AC/2 = CE/3$.

(The fact that BD = BC+CD comes from the diagram.) Now plug in the "parts" to get:

$p \cdot AC + p \cdot CE = AC/2 = CE/3$.

A little substituting gets us:

$p \cdot AC + p \cdot (3/2) \cdot AC = AC/2$.

Now you can cancel the AC's and get $p = 1/5$ which is the same as 20%. The answer is (B).

5. Half of the people who showed up to take the SAT one day at the (fictional) PainIsGood Test Center got nauseous and one-third of the people who got nauseous threw up. One-fifth of the people who did <u>not</u> throw up got bits of vomit on their test papers. One-third of the people with vomit on their test papers decided to leave. All of the people who threw up also left. What fraction of prospective test-takers did <u>not</u> leave?

This is a classic string of fractions problem, a bit longer than what you would see on the real test, but the same general idea.

If you decide to use "p" for the total number of people at the PainIsGood Test Center you get:

$(1/2)p = $ nauseous

$(1/3)(1/2)p = (1/6)p = $ threw up

$(5/6)p = $ did not throw up

$(1/5)(5/6)p = (1/6)p = $ bits of vomit

$(1/3)(1/6)p + (1/6)p = (4/18)p = (2/9)p = $ left

Therefore, 7/9 did not leave (E).

<u>Note:</u> You can also dispense with the p and just use the fractions.

6. You have a hundred dollars in dollar bills. You are going to divide it up (unequally) among four people. You want everyone to get a whole number of dollars and you don't want any money left over. To fulfill these conditions, you can divide the money according to which of the following ratios?

I. $4 : 3 : 2 : 1$

II. $10 : 5 : 2 : 1$

III. $9 : 7 : 3 : 1$

Let's try I first. If you divide it 4:3:2:1, how much money does each person get? Use x for the value of one "share" so $4x + 3x + 2x + x = 100$. That means x is 10 and you divide the money $40 : 30 : 20 : 10$.

If you try to divide it as in II, you get a fraction for x so it doesn't work.

In III, x is 5 and you can divide the money, $45 : 35 : 15 : 5$.

So the answer is (D).

<u>Note:</u> The "x-method" works for many ratio problems: A ratio of 3 to 2 really means one is $3x$ and the other is $2x$.

Note: Figure not drawn to scale.

7! On rectangle ACDE point B is one-quarter of the way between points A and C. A trained ant crawls from point B through point A to point E along the edge of the rectangle traveling 10 cm. A second ant crawls from point B through points C and D to point E along the edge of the rectangle traveling 20 cm. What is the ratio of the length to the width of ACDE?

The key here is to make the length (CD) equal to *ns* (with *s*=AB) since you don't know the length to width ratio anymore. Then you set the ratio of the journey of ant #1 to the journey of ant #2 equal to 2 (=20/10) and solve for *n*.

So AB = *s*, AC = 4*s*, BC = 3*s*, CD = *ns*, DE = 4*s*, and AD = *ns*. The first ant crawls $(n+1)s$ =10 cm and the second ant crawls $(n+7)s$ = 20 cm. So $(n+7)/(n+1) = 20/10 = 2$.

Now solve for *n*, get *n*=5 and the ratio of length to width is 5*s*/4*s* or 1.25 (B).

8. The duration of the lunch break for an executive of the fictional Standardized Testing Service (STS) is directly proportional to the number of years the executive has been with the company. Executive A has been with STS for exactly 5 years and takes 2-hour lunch breaks. The lunch breaks of executive B take a whopping 3 hours and 40 minutes. How long has executive B been "working" for STS?

This question should NOT be construed as implying that STS executives are shiftless, lazy, parasitic good-for-nothing thieves who look good in suits but are otherwise useless. After all, STS isn't even real.

Anyway, 60 months gives you 120 minutes of lunch break and you want to know how many months gives you 220 minutes. You can set up a proportion but why bother? 60 is half of 120 so if you get 220 minutes you must have been working 110 months.

That's 9 years and 2 months.

The answer is (C).

9. If $a^2 - a^2b^2 + b^2 = 0$ then the expression below must be equal to which of the following quantities?

$$\frac{1}{\frac{1}{a^2} + \frac{1}{b^2}}$$

Simplify the expression by getting a common denominator for the two fractions on the bottom, adding them, and then flipping the whole thing:

$$\frac{1}{\frac{1}{a^2} + \frac{1}{b^2}} = \frac{1}{\frac{b^2+a^2}{a^2b^2}} = \frac{a^2b^2}{a^2 + b^2}.$$

They gave an equation which can be re-written as:

$$a^2 + b^2 = a^2b^2.$$

So the top and bottom are the same and the answer is 1 or (C).

<u>Note</u>: You could also solve the equality they gave you in the problem statement for a^2 and get:

$$a^2 = \frac{b^2}{b^2 - 1} \implies \frac{1}{a^2} = \frac{b^2 - 1}{b^2} = 1 - \frac{1}{b^2}.$$

Then you substitute this into the expression they want you to simplify and you get 1.

10. If $y = \dfrac{1 - x^2}{1 - \frac{1}{x^2}}$ and $x \neq 0, \pm 1$, which of the following must be true?

Simplify by replacing 1 with x^2/x^2 to get:

$$y = \frac{1 - x^2}{\frac{x^2-1}{x^2}} = x^2 \cdot \frac{1 - x^2}{x^2 - 1}$$

The rule $a - b = -(b - a)$ is useful here and the result is:

$$y = -x^2.$$

Of course, that doesn't solve the problem. But at least now there's a chance. The first thing to notice is that y is always negative because x^2 is always positive.

So A can't be true because the square root of y isn't even defined. It looks like B could never be true because absolute values are always positive. What about C? If the ratio were less than zero, x and y would have to have different signs. But they could both be negative, so C isn't true. And since they could both be fractions, D isn't true either. So it seems like it's E.

But it isn't. The answer is (B). If y is negative then the absolute value of y is $-y$ which is a *positive* number (x^2 in this case).

End of Section

Fractions Tips

You're such good students! What did we learn in this section?

Hard questions sometimes ask you to define your own variable(s).

Convert words to equations.

Use s or x for the smallest distance.

$(x-y) = -(y-x)$.

Be prepared to work with fractions without a calculator.

The fraction that didn't is 1 minus the fraction that did.

Be concrete. If possible, work with definite numbers.

Switch to smaller units like months and minutes.

An expression like -y may or may not be negative.

1 can always be written as a fraction.

$1/(1/a) = a$.

Write neatly.

Memorizing simple fractions is surprisingly useful:

1/2 = 0.5, 1/3 = 0.33, 1/4 = 0.25, 1/5 = 0.2, 1/6 = 0.166, 1/8 = 0.125, 1/9 = 0.111, 2/3 = 0.666, 3/4 = 0.75, 2/5 = 0.4, 3/5 = 0.6, 4/5 = 0.8 are probably the most useful.

Functions

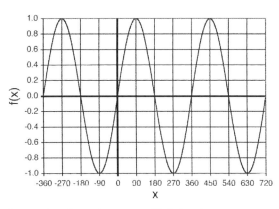

1. The function $y = f(x)$ is shown above. Which of the diagrams below represents the function

$$y = 2f(x+90)+2?$$

When you add 90 inside the function, you shift the function to the left by 90. Think of it this way: To get f(0) with the new function you would have to plug in x=−90.

Doubling the function stretches it vertically: So $2f(x+90)$ goes from −2 to 2.

Adding 2 to the function lifts the whole thing up by 2. So $2f(x+90)+2$ goes from 0 to 4.

So we're looking for a function that is the original function shifted to the left by 90, stretched vertically by a factor of 2, and raised by 2. There will be a bottom at $x = -180$ and a top at $x = 0$. The bottom will be 0 and the top will be 4.

The answer is (A).

In general when you add to the x inside the function as in $f(x+a)$ you shift the function a

units to the left. If you subtract as in $f(x - a)$ you shift the function a units to the right.

Multiplying the function by a positive number as in $Af(x)$ stretches it up and down.

Multiplying the function by a negative number as in $-Af(x)$ flips it around so that what used to be a low point is now a high point. The function gets stretched at the same time.

If A is a fraction, the function gets squeezed vertically instead of stretched. Always keep track of the maximum and minimum values of the old function and the new function.

If you add or subtract from the whole function as in $f(x)+B$ or $f(x)-B$ you just shift the whole thing up or down by B.

The order is as follows: shift left or right, stretch or squeeze, shift up or down. In other words you start inside the $f(x)$ parentheses and work your way out.

They might also throw in something like $f(x) \rightarrow f(-x)$ in which case $f(3)$ switches places with $f(-3)$. This is a reflection with the y-axis as the mirror.

You can also get $f(x) \rightarrow f(2x)$ which means you have to plug in $x = 1/2$ to get the old $f(1)$ point. This is a horizontal squeeze. Note that horizontal squeezes and stretches work kind of backwards — multiplying by 2 causes a horizontal squeeze instead of a stretch. Of course, if you do $f(x) \rightarrow f(x/2)$ that's a horizontal stretch.

2. If $g(x)$ is a quadratic function, which of the diagrams below could be the graph of the following function?
$$y = f(x) = g(x) \cdot (x^3 + 5x^2 + 6x)$$

The unknown $g(x)$ is there to limit the usefulness of your calculator.

You ID the graph by where it crosses the x-axis (the x-axis crossings are called "zeroes" because $f(x)$ is zero at these points).

So when is $f(x)$ equal to zero? Well, obviously when $x=0$. But there are also two other zeroes. We must factor:

$$x^3 + 5x^2 + 6x = x \cdot (x^2 + 5x + 6) = x \cdot (x+2) \cdot (x+3).$$

So $x = 0$, $x = $ -3, and $x = $ -2 all will make $f(x)$ zero.

No matter what $g(x)$ is, the function must be cross the x-axis at these three points. So the answer is (C).

Note 1: With lines or parabolas, setting x to zero and calculating y is often the way to go. That is, you get the y-intercept and ID the function that way. With more complicated functions, the x-intercept is more useful.

Note 2: Since 1 and 2 are also zeroes, $g(x)$ must be some multiple of $(x-1) \cdot (x-2)$.

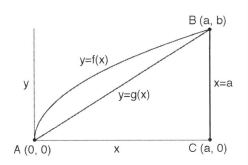

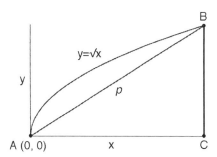

3. In the diagram above, the functions $y = f(x)$ and $y = g(x)$ intersect at points A $(0, 0)$ and B (a, b). The line $x = a$ intersects the x-axis at point C. If c is a number between 0 and a such that $0 \leq c \leq a$, then which of the following must be true?

I. $f(c) - g(c) \geq 0$

II. $f(a/2) > g(c)$

III. The area of $\triangle ABC > \dfrac{c \cdot f(a)}{2}$

No matter what you put in for x, $f(x)$ will always be above $g(x)$. So I is true.

Put your finger halfway between A and C and go up to the function f. That's $f(a/2)$. If you pick a large value of c (close to a) then the $g(c)$ line is definitely above $f(a/2)$. So II is false.

The area of triangle ABC is $a \cdot f(a)/2$; therefore, III would not be true if $c = a$. So III is false and the answer is (A).

4. In the diagram above, line p intersects the curve $y = \sqrt{x}$ at point B and line BC is perpendicular to line AC. The length of line segment AB is $\sqrt{6}$. What is the area of triangle ABC?

If the length of AC is a, point C is $(a, 0)$. The key to this problem is to realize that point B is $(a, \sqrt{a})$. It has to be because point B is on the curve $y = \sqrt{x}$.

Look at the above reasoning carefully and let it sink in. This is the whole key to problems involving intersecting functions.

So now you know that the height of the triangle is $\sqrt{a}$ and the base is a. You also know the pythagorean theorem:

$a^2 + (\sqrt{a})^2 = (\sqrt{6})^2$ or $a^2 + a - 6 = 0$ or $(a + 3)(a - 2) = 0$

You get $a = 2$ ($a=-3$ is nonsense) and do one-half base times height to get $\sqrt{2}$ for the area of the triangle.

The answer is (A).

5. If $f(x) = x^2 + x + 2$ then which of the equations below has the same solution set as $f(x+2) = 4$?

This problem is (purposely) stated in a strange way. They are really asking: "If you plug $(x+2)$ into the function definition and subtract 4, what to you get?"

$f(x+2) = (x+2)^2 + (x+2) + 2 = x^2 + 5x + 8$

So now we have $x^2 + 5x + 8 = 4$ or $x^2 + 5x + 4 = 0$ and that's the answer (B).

---

6. If $f(x) = 4x^2 + 6$ for what value of x does $\dfrac{f(x)}{2} = f(2x)$?

The left side is: $f(x)/2 = 2x^2 + 3$.

For the right side, follow the rule: "square it, multiply by 4, then add 6." You get:

$f(2x) = 4 \cdot (2x)^2 + 6 = 4 \cdot 4x^2 + 6 = 16x^2 + 6$.

Set the left and right side equal, simplify, and get: $14x^2 + 3 = 0$.

It's always tempting to get an answer but there's no way $14x^2$ can be negative. SATAN doesn't use imaginary numbers. The answer is (E).

7. A line with positive slope m intersects the curve $y = x^2 - 2$ at two points with coordinates (a, b) and $(3, c)$. If $a<0$ which of the following contains three possible values of the slope m?

I.   1.5, 2.5, 3.5

II.   1, 2, 3

III.   2, 4, 6

Of course, c is 7 because you can just plug in 3 for x and get $y = 7$. So (3, 7) is one of the two intersection points.

We need to know what slopes are possible given that the slope must be positive (not zero and not negative) and a must be negative.

The point $(a, b) = (-3, 7)$ would give a slope of zero. The point $(a, b) = (0, -2)$ would give a slope of 3. These lines are shown below.

So a is between -3 and 0 (not inclusive) which means the slope of the line connecting (a, b) and (3, 7) is between 0 and 3 (not inclusive).

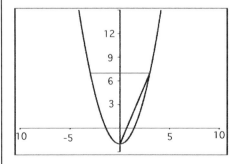

So none of the choices has three possible slopes and the answer is (A).

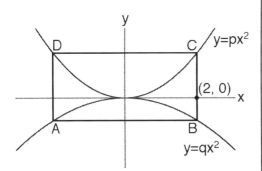

8. Two curves, $y = px^2$ and $y = qx^2$ intersect rectangle ABCD at its four corners. Which of the following expressions gives the area of the rectangle?

The answers all have p and q. The length of the bottom is obviously 4 so all you have to do is get the length of the side (BC) to get the area.

Where is point C? It's at $(2, 4p)$. What's that, magic? No, the x value of point C is 2 and you plug x into the equation of the curve to get the y-value.

In the same way, $(2, 4q)$ is point B. Note that q is negative.

So the length of BC is $4p - 4q$ or $4(p - q)$.

Doing base times height (or length times width) you get $16(p - q)$.

The answer is (E).

Note: With these function/intersection problems you're doing a lot of plugging x into an equation to get y.

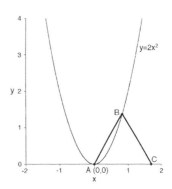

9! The curve $y = 2x^2$ intersects equilateral triangle ABC at vertex A $(0, 0)$ and at vertex B. What is the area of the triangle?

It looks impossible but it isn't. Let's say AB = AC = BC = a.

Point B $\rightarrow (x, 2x^2) = (a/2, 2(a/2)^2) = (a/2, a^2/2)$

Plug in the pythagorean theorem, solve for a, get the area of the triangle, and sleep for a week:

$$(a/2)^2 + (a^2/2)^2 = a^2$$

which means

$$\frac{a^4}{4} = \frac{3}{4}a^2 \implies a = \sqrt{3}$$

So point B is $(\sqrt{3}/2, 3/2)$ which means the area (one half base times height) is:

$$\frac{1}{2} \cdot \sqrt{3} \cdot \frac{3}{2} = \frac{3\sqrt{3}}{4}$$

So the answer is (D).

10. An expensive car containing a number of (fictional) STS executives and their mistresses is moving along a country road at constant speed. The driver is drunk and hits a tree causing the car to stop suddenly (there are several minor injuries and one arrest). Which distance (x) vs. time (t) graph best represents the motion of the car?

Don't be fooled! It's easy to guess wrong on this one. When you answer one like this, you want to ask yourself very clear, concrete questions.

Guesswork is the devil's handmaiden. She may be cute but she is not your friend.

Q. What is the y-axis?

A. Distance.

Q. What is happening to the distance when the car is moving?

A. It is increasing steadily.

Q. What is happening to the distance after the (fictional, drunk) STS executive driver wraps his car around a tree?

A. It stays the same.

These questions make the answer obvious and you get that comforting feeling that you KNOW you are right.

Of course, increasing steadily and then staying the same is represented by (B).

End of Section

Functions Tips

<u>Eff of something is not profanity.</u>

Slope is rise over run.

"f of" means on the curve or line.

$f(x)$ is just another way of saying 'y.'

"Must be true" means "is always true."

If they give you a graph you can often get f(2) (or whatever) just by going over to x=2 and going up till you hit the graph.

$f(x+2) + 3$ shifts the original $f(x)$ graph left 2 and up 3.

Multiplying by 2 as in $2f(x)$ or $2x^2$ makes the original function (in this case $f(x)$ or x^2) taller and narrower.

$f(a)$ might be the height of a triangle or the side of a rectangle.

You can have (a,b) or $(a,f(a))$.

If you know that $y=2x^2$ then any point is $(x,2x^2)$.

Factor to get zeroes to ID a curve.

If a diagram is to scale (*i.e.*, no warning) use it.

Rephrase strange-sounding questions.

Zero is neither positive nor negative.

SATAN may give you a "variable" that can be calculated immediately.

Word Problems

1. Bob and Carol and Ted and Alice are backpacking in the wilderness. Each person carries x pounds of equipment. "Equipment" does not include food, so the total weight of equipment ($4x$) is constant. During the first night, Bob sneaks 10 pounds of equipment from his pack into Carol's. Ted and Alice each sneak 7 pounds of equipment from their packs into Carol's. Later, when the other three are picking berries, Carol divides all the equipment in her pack evenly amongst the packs of her three pals. If Bob's pack now contains 54 pounds of equipment, how much did it contain originally?

Bob starts with x pounds of equipment, gives 10 pounds to Carol and is left with x–10 pounds.

But when Carol gets her revenge, Bob gets one-third of her pack which has the original equipment (x) plus 10 pounds from Bob, 7 pounds from Ted, and 7 pounds from Alice. So Bob gets an extra

$$\frac{x+10+7+7}{3} = \frac{x+24}{3}.$$

added to his pack.

Since Bob ends up with 54 pounds we have:

$$54 = x - 10 + \frac{x+24}{3} \implies 56 = \frac{4}{3}x \implies x = 42.$$

The answer is (D).

2. The area of a triangle is 10 square inches. By how many square inches does the area of the triangle increase if the height is increased by 2 inches while the length of the base remains unchanged?

You don't want to think too much here. The first sentence tells you about a triangle. The second sentence tells you about a changed version of the first triangle. Each sentence is an equation.

First sentence:

$$A_{\text{old}} = \tfrac{1}{2} \cdot b \cdot h = 10.$$

Second sentence:

$$A_{\text{new}} = \tfrac{1}{2} \cdot b \cdot (h+2) = \tfrac{1}{2}bh + b = 10 + b.$$

So the new area is bigger by b square inches.

That's nice but a triangle with an area of 10 could have any base (for example you could have $b = 100$, $h = 0.2$ OR $b = 0.2$, $h = 100$).

We have no idea what the base is.

The answer is (E).

3. Your new motorcycle has a top speed that is 20% faster than the top speed of your old motorcycle. On your old motorcycle it takes you two hours to get to your friend's house traveling at the top speed of the bike (and risking your life for the thrill of speed). How many <u>minutes</u> does the trip take at the top speed of your new motorcycle? Assume, in each case, that you manage to travel at the top speed of the motorcycle for the whole trip (no stop signs, traffic lights *etc.*).

"20% faster" means "multiplied by 1.2."

You have to write $d = rt$ (the "dirt" equation) twice — in this case once for "fast trip" and once for "slow trip."

For the slow trip you get (2 hrs = 120 minutes):

$d = rt = r \cdot 2 = r \cdot 120.$

We don't know the fast trip time so we'll just call it T. We do know the fast trip speed is $1.2r$. Therefore:

$d = 1.2r \cdot T.$

The distance is the same for both trips. So,

$1.2r \cdot T = r \cdot 120 \implies T = 120/1.2 = 100.$

The answer is (A).

<u>Note</u>: You often write d=rt twice. It could be "coming" and "going" or "long trip" and "short trip."

4. After breaking into the headquarters of the fictional Standardized Testing Service (STS) and erasing all their hard drives thereby bringing about a 2-year hiatus from standardized tests, Joe – a fictional hero – is escaping on his motorcycle. Unfortunately, there are a number of fictional, heavily armed STS thugs 10 miles behind him riding specially-built bikes going 150 miles per hour. They are NOT planning to arrest him. If Joe can make it another 50 miles before they catch up to him, he will be able to cross a bridge that will not hold the STS bikes. What minimum average speed in miles per hour must Joe maintain over the next 50 miles to reach the bridge just in the nick of time?

For Joe, the "dirt" equation is: $50 = rt$.

For the thugs: $60 = 150 \cdot t$.

The only thinking/careful reading required was in order to realize that Joe and the thugs go different distances. Otherwise, it's just mechanically writing the two equations.

Now, of course, we just solve the thug equation for t and plug it into Joe's equation.

We get 125 for Joe's speed (E):

$t = 60/150 = 2/5 \implies r = 50 \cdot \dfrac{5}{2} = 125.$

5. When the width and length of a rectangle are each reduced by 20%, the area of the new rectangle is 12 units less than the area of the original rectangle. What is the area of the original rectangle?

"Reduced by 20%" means "multiply by 0.8."

We might as well pick x and y for the width and length of the rectangle.

Now we translate that long nasty sentence:

$0.8x \cdot 0.8y = xy - 12.$

And that's it. We translated everything in the problem and only got one equation with 2 unknowns. If you're panicking, SATAN is laughing.

You calm down and realize that you don't need x and y, all you need is xy. You get:

$12 = xy - .64xy = .36xy \implies xy = 33.3.$

The answer is (C).

<u>Note</u>: You could write:

$A_{\text{old}} = xy$;
$A_{\text{new}} = 0.8x \cdot 0.8y$
$A_{\text{new}} = A_{\text{old}} - 12$;

and then substitute like a maniac but that would be too slow.

6. Square A has an area 30 square meters larger than square B. The perimeter of square A is 8 meters larger than the perimeter of square B. The length in meters of one side of square A is:

Translate the first sentence:

$a^2 = b^2 + 30.$

A good check here is to ask yourself, "Which one is bigger?" Then you say, "A is bigger and you can see that in the equation, good." The danger here of course is putting the 30 on the wrong side.

Now translate the second sentence:

$4a = 4b + 8 \implies a = b + 2.$

Finally, a straight 2 equation, 2 unknown problem. On the SAT these are usually solved by substitution.

In this case:

$(b+2)^2 = b^2 + 30 \implies 4b = 26 \implies b = 6.5.$

Be careful! They wanted a NOT b.

The answer is 8.5 or (C).

<u>Note</u>: Often on the SAT, when you FOIL, the square terms cancel out.

7. The average of two numbers is x. If you multiply one of the numbers by 18, the average of the two new numbers (one of which is unchanged) is $2x$. What is the ratio of the smaller original number to the larger original number?

Here's the translation:

$$\frac{a+b}{2} = x \implies a+b = 2x$$

$$\frac{18a+b}{2} = 2x \implies 18a+b = 4x$$

You don't have enough information to get a or b but that's okay because all they want is a ratio — a over b or b over a, whichever is less than 1.

Double the first equation and substitute for $4x$ to get:

$$18a+b = 2a+2b \implies 16a = b \implies a/b = 1/16$$

So the answer is (B).

Note 1: The ratio of x to y is just x/y. No big deal.

Note 2: Often with average questions you want to actually work with the sum, not the average. The average is just a mean way of telling you the sum.

8. Grandma driving her old car can make it from her house to Las Vegas in 8 hours. If she borrows your car and drives like a maniac, she can make the same trip in 6 hours. Her average speed for the trip in your car is 35 miles per hour faster than her average speed for the trip in her car. What average speed in miles per hour does grandma attain driving your car from her house to Las Vegas?

Another one with 2 "dirt" equations.

Granny's car:

$$d = r \cdot 8.$$

Your car:

$$d = (r+35) \cdot 6.$$

Setting the right sides equal gives:

$$8r = 6r + 210 \implies 2r = 210 \implies r = 105.$$

105 is NOT the answer.

Grandma's speed is $105+35 = 140$.

The answer is (E).

9. In one month Alice-the-lawyer earns half of what her husband, Bill-the-artist, earns in a year (12 months). Together, the happy couple earns 168,000 dollars per year. What is Alice's monthly income in dollars?

This one is rigged up to get you because you have to be very careful keeping track of what the variables mean: is it yearly income or monthly income?

Since the first sentence mentions Alice's monthly income and Bill's yearly income you might pick those as the variables.

Since you are an upstanding, never-do-wrong bookkeeper, you make sure to use a capital letter for Bill's yearly income and a lower case letter for Alice's monthly income.

Alice monthly = m; Bill yearly = B.

Now translate and solve.

1st sentence: $m = \dfrac{1}{2}B \implies B = 2m$

2nd sentence: $12m + B = 168,000$.

Substitute: $12m + 2m = 168,000$.

So $m = 12,000$ and the answer is (A).

10. When Einstein was a small boy, he used to like to blow bubbles. All the bubbles he blew were either big or small. Little Albert always blew his bubbles so that the number of big bubbles was exactly equal to one more than the square root of the number of small bubbles. For one particular bubble-blowing session, the total number of bubbles little Albert blew might have been which of the following? (There is no evidence Einstein ever actually did anything this pointless.)

Translate the third sentence: $B = \sqrt{s} + 1$.

There's no more information so you can't solve it in the usual way because you have one equation with two variables. So it's time for a little trial and error (SATAN loves the fact that this technique is not emphasized at most schools).

You've looked at the answers so you know the total number of bubbles, $B + s$, is in the 40's and you know s has to be a perfect square.

If $s = 36$ then $B = 7$ and the total is 43. If $s = 49$ or if $s = 25$ you get totals that are too big or two small.

The answer is (B).

End of Section

Word Problems Tips

<u>Is this thing a math test or a reading test or what?</u>

The process of translating a word problem (turning the words into equations) is often best done mindlessly like a machine.

Thinking will sometimes (but not always) do nothing but slow you down. For each problem, decide: crunch 'n grind or think.

Distance equals rate times time ("dirt"): $d = rt$

Many "dirt" problems ask you to write $d = rt$ twice.

Convert percents to decimals: 30% = 0.30

Increase by 20% means multiply by 1.2 (DON'T multiply by 0.2 and add).

Decrease by 20% means multiply by 0.8 (DON'T multiply by 0.2 and subtract).

It's not wrong to do percents by multiplying and then adding or subtracting but it's slow and clunky and SATAN purposely makes problems that burn people who do it the long way.

If there's one equation and two unknowns, trial and error might be the only way to solve.

One equation and two unknowns often happens when the unknowns are restricted to integers.

Geometry

Lengths, Angles, Perimeters

circles, regular polygons, sum of angles, parallel lines, triangles, similar triangles, right triangles, algebraic perimeters, symmetry

Areas

inscribed circles, inscribed triangles, inscribed squares, shaded regions, symmetry, sectors of circles

Triangles

symmetry, possibility problems (length, angles, areas), 30-60-90, 45-45-90, isosceles triangles, equilateral triangles, inscribed equilateral triangles

Points and Space

xy coordinates, possible areas, lines that form figures, possible distances given constraints (locus problems), mental rotations and manipulations

Lengths, Angles, Perimeters

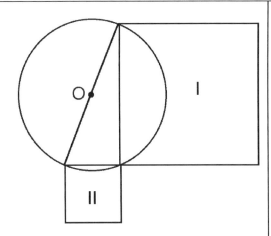

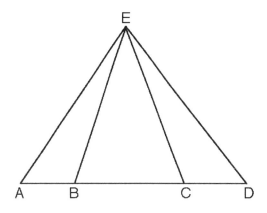

Note: Figure not drawn to scale.

1. The area of circle O is 20π. The sum of the areas of square I and square II is:

If they give you a circle the first thing to do is get the radius:

$$\pi r^2 = 20\pi \implies r = \sqrt{20}.$$

You've got a right triangle so you're almost certainly going to use pythagorean theorem. Even if you aren't sure what to do, you can just plug it in and see what you get.

Label one side of square I with an a; label square II with a b. Pythagorus (he's dead) says:

$$a^2 + b^2 = \left(2\sqrt{20}\right)^2 = 4 \cdot 20 = 80.$$

That's the answer since $a^2 + b^2$ happens to be the sum of the areas of the squares.

The answer is (B).

2. In the figure above, AE=DE and BE=CE. The area of triangle AED is 5 times the area of triangle BEC. What is the ratio of the length of AB to the length of BC?

Since the area of triangle AED is 5 times bigger than BEC and the heights are the same, we know that AD is 5 times longer than BC.

Now we need a ratio but we don't know much about the length of AB so it seems like it can't be done. SATAN loves that.

With ratio problems, putting in an x is always a good idea. In this case, we say BC = x and AD = $5x$.

Suddenly you see that AB = CD = $2x$. They have to be equal because of the symmetry in the problem (SATAN likes symmetry). Of course, $2x + x + 2x = 5x$.

So the ratio is 2 and the answer is (D).

3! Line *l* is tangent to circle O at point (*a*, *b*) and *a*>0 and *b*>0. If the center of circle O is at the origin and if circle O consists of all points (*x*, *y*) such that $x^2 + y^2 = 10$ which of the following expressions gives the *y*-intercept of line *l*?

This one is pretty vicious especially without a diagram. Of course, it's best to draw your own.

The crucial fact here is that the radius drawn to a tangent is perpendicular to the tangent. This means the slope of the tangent is the negative reciprocal of the slope of the radius.

Remember, with circle problems, always draw a convenient radius.

Okay, so the slope of the radius drawn to point (*a*, *b*) is rise/run = *b*/*a*. You've already noticed that the answers have *a*'s and *b*'s in them.

The slope of the tangent is -*a*/*b*. The equation of the tangent line is the usual *y* = *mx* + *c*. Note that we have used *c* for the *y*-intercept instead of the usual *b* because there's already a *b* in the problem (SATAN is laughing his head off).

So now we plug in the slope for *m* and the point (*a*, *b*) for *x* and *y* and solve for *c* and we're done. We get:

$$b = -\frac{a}{b} \cdot a + c \implies b^2 + a^2 = cb \implies c = \frac{10}{b}$$

So the answer is (A).

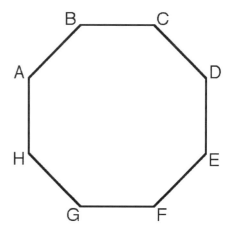

4. Regular octagon ABCDEFGH has sides of length *s*. What is the length of AD in terms of *s*?

Label the sides with an *s* and draw AD. It's an octagon so each angle is 180–(360/8) or 135 degrees.

Remember, IT HAS TO BE EASY. Otherwise SATAN couldn't put it on the test.

There must something simple in the problem like a 45-45-90 triangle. If you draw a perpendicular from point B to line AD you get your 45-45-90 triangle. Now you can get $s/\sqrt{2}$ for one piece of AD, *s* for the middle piece, and $s/\sqrt{2}$ for the other piece. The length of AD is:

$$AD = \frac{s}{\sqrt{2}} + s + \frac{s}{\sqrt{2}} = \frac{2s}{\sqrt{2}} + s = s\sqrt{2} + s = s(\sqrt{2} + 1)$$

The answer is (B).

<u>Moral</u>: If thou art lost, seek ye the easy triangle (and remember $1/\sqrt{2} = \sqrt{2}/2$).

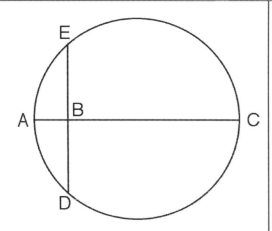

Note: Figure not drawn to scale.

5. In the diagram above, AC is a diameter of the circle, AB=2, BC=8, and DE is perpendicular to AC. What is the length of DE?

If you are given a circle, always draw at least one radius (pick one that is likely to be useful) and figure out how long it is if you can.

In this case, the radius is 5 since AC = 8+2 = 10.

Which radius did you draw? How about drawing lines from the center to points E and D and making some beautiful right triangles?

The distance from B to the center is 3 (because the radius is 5 and AB=2). That means you have a two 3-4-5 triangles (SATAN loves these). Both BE and BD are 4 which means DE = 8.

The answer is (C).

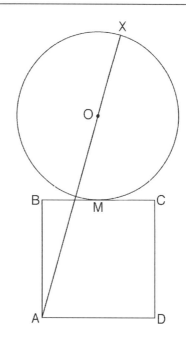

6. In the diagram above, circle O has a diameter of 20. Line segment BC is tangent to circle O at point M and M is the midpoint of BC. If ABCD is a square and if line segment AB has length 14, what is the length of line segment AX?

It's the famous "there's a line not in the figure that you have to draw and if you don't you're screwed" problem.

What you want is a nice right triangle, so you draw the line from point O through point M all the way down to the midpoint of AD.

Your brilliant line has length 10 + 14 = 24 and half of AD is 7 so you've got yourself a 7, 24, 25 triangle. That is, AO is 25.

Since OX is 10, the answer is 35 or (E).

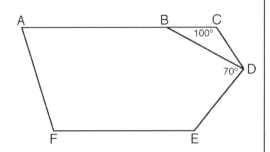

Note: Figure not drawn to scale.

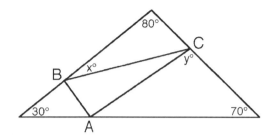

Note: Figure not drawn to scale.

7. In the figure above, AC is parallel to EF, BC=CD, angle BCD=100°, and angle BDE=70°. What is the measure in degrees of angle FED?

Since BCE is 100 and the triangle is isosceles, the little angles must be 40. This means CDE is 70+40 =110.

It's a five-sided figure so A+C+CDE+E+F=540. We're trying to get E (that is, FED) but we don't know A and we don't know F.

This is one of SATAN's favorite tricks. You DON'T need to know angles A and F. Since the lines are parallel (a fact we haven't used yet), the SUM of A and F is 180. If FED = x and we start with angle BCD and go around clockwise we get:

$100 + 110 + x + 180 = 540 \implies x = 150.$

The answer is (D).

Note: 3 sides: 180°; 4 sides: 360°; 5 sides: 540°; 6 sides: 720°; 8 sides: 1080°

8. In the figure above, $\triangle$ABC is a right triangle with AB $= \sqrt{2}$, AC $= \sqrt{6}$. If $y = 100 - x$, what is the value of x?

The thing that looks like a 30-60-90 really is one because AC = $\sqrt{3}$ times AB.

Now you put everything you know into the diagram and hope for the best. It is *not* necessary to see the light at the end of the tunnel.

There are a number of places to start (and they'll all work). We'll start at y.

You can cross out y and write 100–x where the y was (this was given). The little angle next to y is 30 degrees so you write that in. The next angle that has C as a vertex is 100–x because it's part of a triangle with angles x and 80° (triangle has to add to 180).

Now you have 3 angles, 100–x, 30, and 100–x, which make a straight line which means they add up to 180. Solving 230–2x = 180 gives x=25.

The answer is (A).

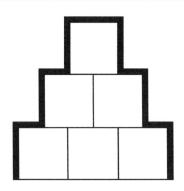

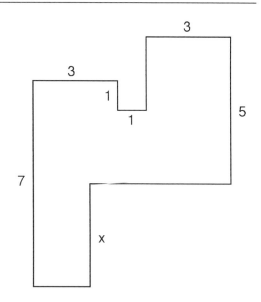

9! The child of an STS executive builds a pyramid out of *N* identical cubical blocks (*N* = 6 is shown). The child says "Daddy, daddy, the outside edge of the front face of my pyramid (shown in bold) measures 300 cm and each of my blocks has a volume of 125 cubic cm; guess how many blocks are in my pyramid!" The STS executive has no idea but he saves the question for a future test. What is the value of *N*?

If the pyramid has *l* levels and the blocks have side *s* then the bold line is $3ls$ (there's an *ls* going up, an *ls* going down, and an *ls* going sideways).

$3ls = 15l$ because the sides are the cube root of 125 which gives $s = 5$.

Since the kid told us that the bold line is 300 there must be 20 levels ($15l = 300$).

The number of blocks in a 20-level pyramid is $1+2+3+ \ldots +19+20 = (20){\cdot}(20+1)/2 = 210$. The answer is (D).

10! If all line segments in the figure shown above are either vertical or horizontal, which of the following gives the perimeter of the figure in terms of *x*?

Starting from the lower left corner, we see that $7+3+1+1+1+godknowswhat+3+5+x+thebottom$ is the perimeter of the figure.

Fortunately, *thebottom* has to be 7 (we don't care about the individual lengths!).

The problem is, what is *godknowswhat*? Well it's the amount by which the top right is higher than the top left but that's not much help.

Here's the trick: $5 + x = 7 + godknowswhat$. This means $godknowswhat = x - 2$ and the perimeter is $26 + 2x$ or (E).

End of Section

Lengths, Angles, Perimeters Tips

You need to know this for day-to-day life. Really.

Look for 3-4-5, 6-8-10, 9-12-15, 5-12-13, 10-24-26, 7-24-25, 8-15-17, and 20-21-29 triangles.

A lot of answers are in terms of π.

Angles of a triangle add up to 180.

Parallel lines: alternate interior and corresponding angles are congruent; same side interiors add up to 180.

The tangent to a circle is perpendicular to the radius.

The slope of a perpendicular is the negative reciprocal of the original.

The slope of a radius drawn from the origin to the point (x, y) is y/x.

Central angles are 72, 60, 45 for regular pentagon, hexagon, octagon.

Sum of interior angles are 540, 720, and 1080 for 5-sided, 6-sided, and 8-sided figures.

With circle problems, draw a convenient radius and get its length.

45-45-90 is $1 : 1 : \sqrt{2}$ or $1/\sqrt{2} : 1/\sqrt{2} : 1$; 30-60-90 triangle is $1 : \sqrt{3} : 2$

If there's something in the problem you would like to know, make a variable for it and put it in the diagram.

Draw lines to make convenient right triangles.

"Five times bigger" means x and 5x in the diagram.

If you have two unknown angles or sides, consider that you may just need their sum. This is a favorite ploy of SATAN.

Areas

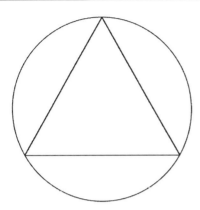

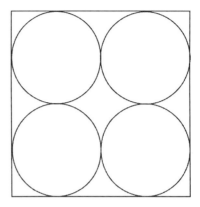

1. An equilateral triangle is inscribed in a circle with radius 2. What is the area of the triangle?

It's equilateral so all the angles are 60.

Of course, since this is the SAT, the trick is to draw lines and make a 30-60-90 triangle.

Of course, you've memorized the ratio of side lengths:

30-60-90 ratio: $1 : \sqrt{3} : 2$.

To make your triangle, draw the radius from the center of the circle to a corner and draw a line from the center perpendicular to a side.

The radius is your hypotenuse and it is 2. This makes the height 1 and the base equal to $\sqrt{3}$.

The area of your 30-60-90 is one-half base times height or $\sqrt{3}/2$. Since there are six of these little triangles in your big triangle, the area of the big triangle is $3\sqrt{3}$.

The answer is (A).

2. The area of the square in the diagram is equal to s^2. The four circles have equal radii and are tangent to each other and to the sides of the square. What fraction of the area of the square is occupied by the four circles?

Each side of the square must have length s. The radius of each circle is therefore $s/4$ so the total area of all four circles is:

$4 \cdot \pi r^2 = 4 \cdot \pi (s/4)^2 = 4\pi s^2/16 = \pi s^2/4$.

"Fraction of its area" means the area of the four circles divided by the total area of the square:

Area ratio $= \dfrac{\pi s^2/4}{s^2} = \dfrac{\pi}{4}$.

So the answer is (E).

<u>Note</u>: Technically, they could ask a question like this without giving you s. The side length cancels out, so this answer is true for *any* square with four circles in it.

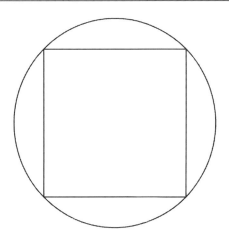 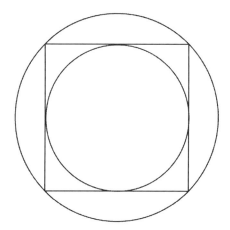

3. A square is inscribed in a circle. The area of the circle is 6. What is the area of the square?

With circle problems the first step is almost always to draw a convenient radius and try to get its value. The area gives you the radius:

$$6 = \pi r^2 \implies r = \sqrt{6/\pi}.$$

In this case, the most convenient radius is the one drawn to the corner of the square. This radius is the hypotenuse of a 45-45-90 triangle. You know how to get the legs from the radius:

$$\text{legs} = \frac{\text{hypotenuse}}{\sqrt{2}} = \frac{\sqrt{6/\pi}}{\sqrt{2}} = \sqrt{3/\pi}$$

Since the side of the square is just twice one of the legs, the area of the square is:

$$\text{Area} = (2\sqrt{3/\pi})^2 = 4 \cdot (3/\pi) = 12/\pi.$$

The answer is (C).

4. A square is inscribed in a large circle. A small circle is inscribed in the square. If the area of the small circle is 1, what is the area of the large circle?

Again, you've got the area of the small circle so you can get its radius:

$$1 = \pi r^2 \implies r = \sqrt{1/\pi}.$$

If you draw the small radius perpendicular to the side of the square and the big radius to a corner of the square you get a nice 45-45-90 triangle.

This time you've got the leg and want the hypotenuse so:

$$\text{hypotenuse} = \text{leg} \cdot \sqrt{2} = \sqrt{1/\pi} \cdot \sqrt{2} = \sqrt{2/\pi}.$$

This is the radius of the big circle so:

$$\text{Area} = \pi \cdot R^2 = \pi \cdot \left(\sqrt{2/\pi}\right)^2 = 2.$$

The answer is (D).

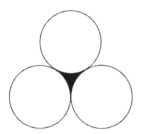

5. Each circle in the figure above has radius $r=1$. What is the area of the shaded region surrounded by the three circles?

First, you have to draw six convenient radii. In this case, you end up with an equilateral triangle connecting the centers of the three circles.

The area of the shaded region is the area of the equilateral triangle minus the area of the three 60-degree sectors. Each sector is one-sixth of the area of its circle.

Draw the height of the equilateral triangle to make two 30-60-90 triangles. The hypotenuse is 2, the short leg is 1, and the long leg (the height) is $\sqrt{3}$. The area is:

$$A_{\text{equilateral triangle}} = \tfrac{1}{2}bh = \tfrac{1}{2} \cdot 2 \cdot \sqrt{3} = \sqrt{3}.$$

The area of each circle is π, the area of one sector is $\pi/6$, and the total area of all three sectors is $\pi/2$.

Now subtract the sector areas from the equilateral triangle area to get the shaded region:

$$A_{\text{shaded}} = A_{\text{triangle}} - A_{\text{sectors}} = \sqrt{3} - \frac{\pi}{2} = \frac{2\sqrt{3} - \pi}{2}.$$

The answer is (D).

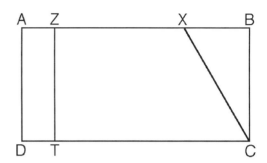

6. In the figure above, ZX/AB = 4/7. If the area of rectangle AZTD is equal to the area of triangle BCX and if the area of quadrilateral AXCD = 30, what is the area of rectangle ABCD?

Since ZX / AB = 4/7 you can just say ZX = 4 and AB = 7 as long as it doesn't contradict the given information (8 and 14 would work just fine too).

If a rectangle has the same area and height as a triangle, the base of the triangle has to be twice the base of the rectangle (think about this).

So AZ is 1 and XB is 2 (AZ + ZX + XB = 7).

They didn't give us BC so we'll just call it y and start writing equations and hope it works out (you don't have to see the light at the end of the tunnel).

The area of ABCD is $7y$. The area of triangle BCX is y. Since the area of AXCD is 30:

$$30 = 7y - y = 6y \implies y = 5.$$

So the area of ABCD is $7 \cdot 5 = 35$ (B).

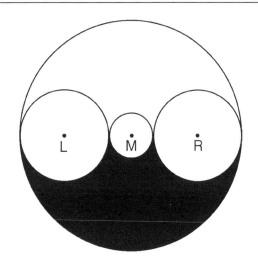

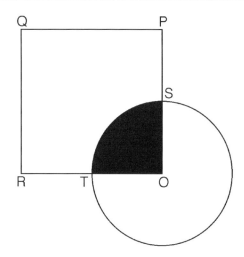

7. The largest and smallest circles in the diagram are concentric with center M. Circles L and R are tangent to the smallest circle and to the largest circle and each has a radius equal to twice the radius of the smallest circle. Line segment LMR lies on the diameter of the largest circle. The area of the shaded region is 16π. What is the radius of the smallest circle?

It would be easier if they gave us the radius and asked for the area. Oh well. We'll have to put in the area they gave us and solve for r.

$A_{\text{small circles}} = \pi \cdot r^2 + \pi \cdot (2r)^2 + \pi \cdot (2r)^2 = 9\pi r^2$.

The shaded area is the half of the what's left after you do big circle (radius = 5r) minus small circles:

$A_{\text{shaded}} = \frac{1}{2}(25\pi r^2 - 9\pi r^2) = 8\pi r^2 = 16\pi \implies r = \sqrt{2}$

So the answer is (B).

8. The center of circle O is one of the vertices of square OPQR. The midpoint of OP is S and the midpoint of OR is T. The shaded region occupies what fraction of the square?

Let's say the square is s by s. That means the radius of the circle is $s/2$.

The area of the circle is $\pi s^2/4$ and the area of the shaded region (a quarter of the circle) is $\pi s^2/16$.

So the area of the shaded region divided by the area of the square is $\pi/16$.

The answer is (D).

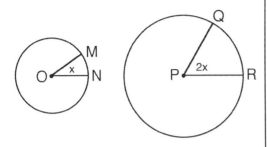

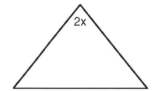

Note: Figure not drawn to scale.

Note: Figure not drawn to scale.

9. The area of circle P is twice that of circle O. The measure of angle MON is equal to x. The measure of angle QPR is equal to $2x$. If the clockwise distance along circle O from point M to point N is equal to 3, what is the clockwise distance along circle P from point Q to point R?

If you double the area of a circle, you multiply the radius by $\sqrt{2}$. For example, if the radius of a circle is 1, its area is π. If the radius of a circle is $\sqrt{2}$, its area is 2π.

If you start with circle O and double the area, you multiply the radius, circumference, and all arc lengths by $\sqrt{2}$. So arc MN would become $3\sqrt{2}$.

To make arc QR, you then double the angle. This doubles the arc length. So arc QR is $6\sqrt{2}$.

The answer is (B).

10! An isosceles triangle has vertex angle $x<90°$ and an area equal to 2. A new isosceles triangle is drawn with vertex angle $2x$. If the new triangle has the same height as the original triangle, the area of the new triangle is:

The question is asking, "what happens to the base of the triangle if you double the angle?" For very small angles (say $x = 1°$) the base of the triangle is about the same as the arc length of a circle centered at the vertex. Doubling a small angle would exactly double the arc length of the circle and would approximately double the length of the base of the triangle.

What about a large angle like 89.9999 degrees? If you double this angle you will get a REALLY long base. In fact, if the angle x is very close to 90°, the base of the triangle can be as long as you want: it could be 10 times longer than the original base or 100 times longer or even more.

So the answer is "cannot be determined" or (E).

End of Section

Areas Tips

Why would anyone shade that particular region?

If there's a circle, job 1 is to get the radius.

If you have a square in a circle, draw a radius to a corner of the square.

If you have a circle in a square, draw a radius parallel to the side of the square.

If you double the radius of a circle, you quadruple the area but only double the circumference.

Sector angle doubles means area and arc length both double because you are doubling the fraction of the "pie" occupied by the sector.

A 120 degree sector is 1/3 of the circle; 90 degrees is 1/4 of the circle; 72 degrees is 1/5 of the circle; 60 degrees is 1/6; 45 degrees is 1/8; 36 degrees is 1/10; 30 degrees is 1/12 of the circle.

Memorize: 45-45-90 is $x : x : x\sqrt{2}$ and 30-60-90 is $x : x\sqrt{3} : 2x$.

Know area (πr^2) and circumference ($2\pi r$) formulas cold. Also know volume ($\pi r^2 \cdot h$) and lateral surface area ($2\pi r \cdot h$) of a cylinder.

To double the area of a circle you multiply the radius by the square root of 2 (that's because you square the radius to get the area).

Don't be afraid to label an unknown side with a variable.

A length ratio like 4/7 goes into the diagram as 4x and 7x or maybe even as 4 and 7.

Triangles

1. What is the largest possible area in square cm of a right triangle whose hypotenuse measures 6 cm?

The easiest way to do this is to use the "biggest means most symmetric" trick. In this case, the biggest right triangle is the one where the two legs are equal.

If the two legs are equal then they are both equal to 6/√2 because it is a 45-45-90.

The area is one-half base times height or

$$A = \frac{1}{2} \cdot \frac{6}{\sqrt{2}} \cdot \frac{6}{\sqrt{2}} = \frac{36}{4} = 9.$$

So the answer is (B).

Note: To prove this you could imagine that the hypotenuse is the diameter of a circle and that you are making your right triangle by inscribing it in the circle as in the diagram below. The largest height you can get is the radius which is 3. The area is one half base times height which equals 9.

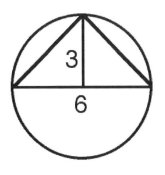

2. In triangle ABC, AB is chosen as the base. The height of the triangle with AB as the base is h and h=AB. Which of the following is true?

I. △ABC could be a right triangle.

II. Angle C cannot be a right angle.

III. Angle C could be less than 45°.

For I, all you need is a right triangle with equal base and height. That's no problem.

For II, draw a right triangle with right angle C. The base AB is the hypotenuse. The height is a perpendicular line drawn from point C to AB and is definitely shorter than AB. So if C is a right angle, the height can't be equal to AB. Therefore C cannot be a right angle and II is true.

For III, you have to remember that the height can be *outside* of the triangle. Angle C can be as small as you like as in the diagram below.

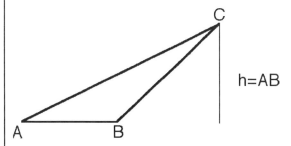

So III is also true and the answer is (E).

3. If triangle XYZ is not a right triangle then a line drawn from vertex Z to side XY that is perpendicular to XY is <u>always</u>:

The perpendicular from a point to a line is the shortest distance from the point to the line so it is shorter than XZ and shorter than YZ.

The answer is (D).

<u>Note</u>: In a right triangle, two sides are perpendicular to each other so the perpendicular from two of the vertices to the opposite side *is* one of the sides. That's why the question had to stipulate that it wasn't a right triangle if the answer was going to be that the perpendicular is always shorter.

4. The length of each of the sides of a triangle is a positive integer and n is a positive integer. If the length of one side is $n+10$ and the length of another side is $n+12$, then the <u>shortest</u> possible length of the third side is:

The two short sides have to add up to *more* than the long side or you can't draw the triangle.

(If the two short sides added up to *exactly* the long side, then when you tried to draw the triangle, it would be totally flat — just a straight line.)

So the short side has be more than 2 and it has to be an integer so the shortest possible third side is 3.

The answer is (E).

<u>Note</u>: The *longest* possible third side would be $2n+21$.

5. A line segment is drawn from the origin to point A (4, 3). Another line segment is drawn perpendicular to the first from point A to point B $(b, 0)$ on the x-axis. What is the value of b?

The slope of the first line is rise/run = 3/4. The slope of the second line is -4/3 because it is perpendicular to the first.

The equation of the second line is the same old $y = mx + c$ and we have to use c for the y-intercept because there's a b in the problem.

We know the line goes through (4,3) so we know that $3 = -(4/3)\cdot 4 + c$. This means $c = 25/3$.

Now we can find the x-intercept by setting y equal to zero in the equation for the line:

$$0 = -\frac{4}{3}x + \frac{25}{3} \implies x = \frac{25}{4} = 6.25.$$

The x-intercept is (6.25, 0). The answer is (A).

Note: Here's a faster way. The slope of the line from (4,3) to $(b,0)$ is $-4/3$. This slope is also $-3/d$. Therefore,

$$-\frac{4}{3} = -\frac{3}{d} \implies d = \frac{9}{4} = 2.25 \implies b = 6.25.$$

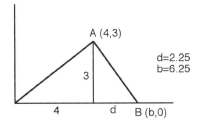

A (4,3)

d=2.25
b=6.25

3

4   d   B (b,0)

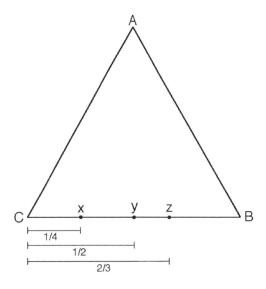

6. Triangle ABC is equilateral and BC=1. Another equilateral triangle is to be inscribed in ABC so that each side of triangle ABC contains one vertex of the inscribed triangle. Which of the three points along BC in the figure may be used as a vertex of the inscribed equilateral triangle?

If you start at point x, you go to the point on AC that is 1/4 unit from point A. Then you go to the point on AB that is 1/4 unit from point B. Will all sides be equal? If one was bigger than the others, which would it be? Since there is no answer to that question, the three sides must be equal.

The same reasoning works for points y and z. So all three points, x, y, and z, can be used to make an equilateral triangle.

The answer is (E).

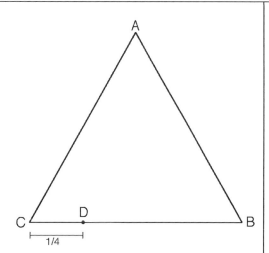

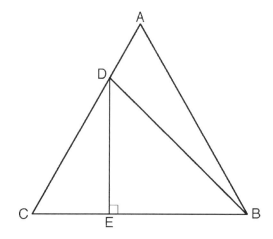

Note: Figure not drawn to scale.

7. Triangle ABC is equilateral and BC=1. A line segment is to be drawn from point D to AC. If the line segment intersects AC at point E, what is the shortest possible length of DE?

Since ABC is equilateral, all the angles (A, B, and C) are 60.

The shortest possible line from point D to AC is a line perpendicular to AC. Label the intersection point E.

Triangle DCE is 30-60-90 with hypotenuse DC = 1/4. The length of the short leg CE is half the hypotenuse or 1/8. The length of the long leg is √3 times the length of the short leg or √3/8.

The answer is (E).

8. Triangle ABC is equilateral. If BE=DE and DE is perpendicular to BC, what is the ratio of the length of CE to the length of BC?

It's good to put the information from the problem statement into the diagram. So you should label all the angles you know (there's a 60, a 30, and a couple of 45's to label).

They are asking for a ratio so you don't have to actually get the length of anything. If one side is x, all the other sides are based on that one, and x cancels out of any ratio.

So you label CE with an x. Triangle DCE is 30-60-90. So DE is $x\sqrt{3}$. You also have a 45-45-90 triangle (DBE) so BE is also $x\sqrt{3}$. Therefore:

$$\frac{CE}{BC} = \frac{x}{x+x\sqrt{3}} = \frac{x}{x(1+\sqrt{3})} = \frac{1}{1+\sqrt{3}}.$$

The answer is (D).

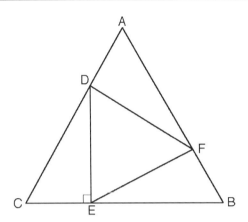

Note: Figure not drawn to scale.

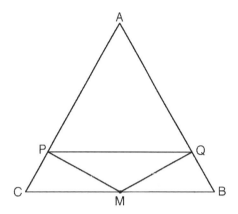

Note: Figure not drawn to scale.

9. Triangle ABC is equilateral. If triangle DEF is also equilateral and DE is perpendicular to BC, what is the ratio of the length of CE to the length of BC?

The quickest way is to label all the angles and realize that there are three equal 30-60-90 triangles (DCE, EBF, and FAD). They have to be equal because of symmetry (if one were bigger which would it be?).

So if CE is x then FB is also x. Since EB is the hypotenuse of a 30-60-90, it must be $2x$.

Therefore:

$$\frac{CE}{BC} = \frac{x}{x+2x} = \frac{1}{3}.$$

The answer is (A).

10! Triangle ABC is still equilateral. If M is the midpoint of BC and MP and MQ are perpendicular to AC and AB, what is the ratio of the length of PQ to the length of BC?

It's often easiest to pick a short side as your x so you don't get a lot of fractions. So pick PC=x.

Since MCP is 30-60-90 and the short side is x, we get that the hypotenuse MC=$2x$ which means MB also equals $2x$ and BC=$4x$.

We know AC is also $4x$ because ABC is equilateral and this lets us label AP with a $3x$. Almost done. By symmetry, PQ is parallel to BC which makes APQ equilateral and PQ equal to $3x$.

The ratio PQ/BC = $3x/4x = 3/4$.

The answer is (D).

End of Section

Triangles Tips

<u>When does a triangle have four sides?</u>

The area of a triangle is one half base times height.

You can draw 3 heights for any triangle.

The height is perpendicular to the base.

The height can be outside the triangle.

If you know an angle or a length put it in the diagram.

The two short sides of a triangle have to add up to more than the long side (otherwise the short sides wouldn't be able to reach each other).

Equilateral: 60-60-60 and 1 : 1 : 1

30-60-90 is 1 : $\sqrt{3}$: 2

45-45-90 is 1 : 1 : $\sqrt{2}$

To get a ratio of two sides, label one side with an *x* and try to get the other side in terms of *x*.

The slope of a perpendicular line is the negative reciprocal of the slope of the original line.

Don't use *b* for the intercept if there's already a *b* in the problem.

Modern SAT questions sometimes insist that you draw a diagram as a prelude to solving the problem (in the old days, they almost always gave you a diagram if one was needed).

Points and Space

1. A rectangular prism measures 3 cm by 4 cm by 5 cm. Points A and B are different points on the surface of this solid. What is the largest possible length of line segment AB?

This is the classic 3D pythagorean theorem problem which they ask in many guises. The basic equation is:

$$a^2 + b^2 + c^2 = d^2.$$

For this problem, the largest possible distance is the distance from one corner of the rectangular prism (it's really just a box) through the center of the box to the opposite corner. (This is called the "body diagonal.")

Do 3D pythagorean and get:

$$3^2 + 4^2 + 5^2 = 50 = d^2 \implies d = \sqrt{50} = 5\sqrt{2}.$$

The answer is (C).

<u>Note</u>: Look for this with any question that has a cube or rectangular prism. SATAN asks it and re-asks it and tries to disguise it each time. For example, the body diagonal of a cube is also the diameter of a sphere around the cube.

2. What is the area of the triangle formed by the x-axis, the line $y = x$, and the line $y = -\frac{1}{2}x + 3$?

You must draw a diagram. The x-axis is easy enough. The line $y = x$ goes up and to the right at a 45 degree angle with the positive x-axis. The line $y = -(1/2)x + 3$ starts at the point $y = 3$ and goes down and to the right. This line hits the x-axis at x=6 (y=0).

The base is obviously 6 (from 0,0 to 0,6).

To get the height, you need to figure out the y coordinate of the point where the two lines intersect. The easiest way is to substitute $x = y$ into $y = -(1/2)x + 3$ to get $y = -(1/2)y + 3$. Now you can solve for y and get $y = 2$.

So the base is 6 and the height is 2. This means the area is 6 and the answer is (B).

3! A rectangle has a perimeter of 20 inches. Which of the following could be the area of this rectangle in square inches?

    I.   8

    II.   23

    III.   26

We are given that $l+w$ is 10. Try $(l,w) = (9,1)$ or $(8,2)$ or $(7,3)$ or $(6,4)$ or $(5,5)$. The area gets bigger and bigger and hits its maximum at $(5,5)$.

The area can be as small as you like (a very long, very skinny rectangle) but it tops out at 25. So 8 and 23 are possible but 26 is too big.

The answer is (C).

<u>Note</u>: To prove 26 is no good you can write $lw=26$ and $l+w=10$, eliminate w, and get:

$$l \cdot (10-l) = 26 \implies l^2 - 10l + 26 = 0$$

which has no solution because

$$b^2 - 4ac = 100 - 4 \cdot 26 < 0.$$

4. Points A and B on plane P are 5 units apart. How many points in plane P are <u>both</u> 3 units from point B <u>and</u> 6 units from point A?

All the points 3 units from point B are on a circle with radius 3 with point B at the center.

All the points 6 units from point A are on a circle with radius 6 with point A at the center.

Draw points A and B and two circles on a diagram reasonably to scale and you see two intersection points. These intersection points are the 2 points that are 3 units from B and 6 units from A.

So the answer is (C).

5. Points A and B on plane P are 5 inches apart. How many points in plane P are 4 inches from point B and <u>more than</u> 4 inches from point A?

Again, draw two circles both with radius 4 around points A and B.

There is a whole section of the circle around B that is outside of the circle around A. All of the points (an infinite number) on this section are 4 inches from B and more than 4 inches from A.

So the answer is (E).

6. Points A and B are 6 inches apart. Point M is the midpoint of AB. Point C is 4 inches from point M and point D is 2 inches from point B. Points A, B, C, D, and M all lie on a plane. Which of the following could be the length of CD in inches?

I. 0

II. 1

III. 9

First draw the diagram below with a radius 4 circle centered at M to represent all the possible points C and a radius 2 circle centered at B to represent all the possible points D.

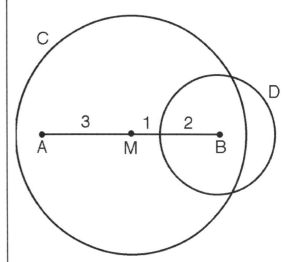

Since the circles intersect, CD could be zero. The distance from the rightmost point on the D circle to the leftmost point on the C circle is 9 so CD could be anything between 0 and 9.

The answer is (E).

7. Points A, B, C, and D lie on a plane. The distance between points A and B is 24, AC=BC=15, and AD=BD=13. Which of the following could be the distance between points C and D in inches?

I.   4

II.   9

III. 14

To get this one, we need to first draw the diagram below. Note that points C and D could be on the same side of AB or on the opposite side.

Points A, C, and the midpoint of AB make two 9-12-15 right triangles (a multiple of 3-4-5).

There are also four 5-12-13 triangles.

There are two possible lengths of CD: 4 and 14 (=9+5).

So the answer is (D).

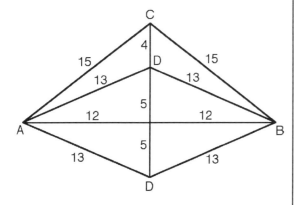

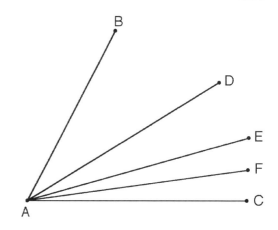

8. In a the diagram above, line segment AD bisects angle BAC, line segment AE bisects angle DAC, and line segment AF bisects angle EAC. Angle BAC is less than 90 degrees. If all angles less than 90 degrees and greater than 0 degrees in the diagram are measured, including overlapping and non-overlapping angles, how many numerically different results will be obtained?

Suppose we say BAC measures 1 unit. The smallest angle, FAC, would be 1/8 and all of the possible angles would be some number of eighths.

BAF is 7/8; BAE is 6/8; BAD is 4/8; DAF is 3/8; and DAE is 2/8.

There's no way to make 5/8.

Including BAC (8/8) and FAC (1/8), there are 7 different angles possible so the answer is (D).

red	pink
blue	gray

9. The card represented above is painted a different color in each of four quadrants as shown. It is rotated $x°$ counter-clockwise about an axis perpendicular to the plane of the card and passing through its center. Which of the cards below could NOT represent the result of this rotation?

The hard way is to visualize the counter-clockwise rotations. (A) is 270°, (B) is 90°, (D) is 180°, and (E) is 360°.

No rotation, clockwise or counter-clockwise will get (C).

If you look at the card above and move clockwise from red to pink to blue to gray you get something that won't change no matter how you rotate the card: the order of the colors.

If you start from red and go clockwise around the card you *always* get red-pink-gray-blue even if it was rotated.

If you go clockwise from red on choice (C) you get red-blue-gray-pink. The only way to get choice (C) from the card above would be to switch the pink and blue squares without moving the red and gray squares. But you can't do this by rotating the card.

The answer is (C).

10. A cube has a different letter on each face. The letters are A, B, C, D, E, and F. Another cube is similar except that the letters on the faces are A, B, C, G, H, and I. Both cubes are opaque. The cubes are glued together face-to-face and set down on an opaque table. If the cubes are not moved, what is the <u>minimum</u> number of <u>different</u> letters that must be visible to a person who walks around the table? (The person can see all of the exposed faces.)

To get the minimum number of letters you have to imagine trying to cover up as many letters as possible. You want to stay away from covering up A, B, or C because if you glue a C face to a C face, you've only covered up one letter. If you glue a C face to a B face, you haven't covered up any letters because there is another B face and another C face.

The way to cover up the most letters is to glue a D face to a G face and then place the blocks so that the E and H faces are on the opaque table. That way only A, B, C, F, and I will be visible. In general you should pick 4 of the six letters D, E, F, G, H, I to cover up. Five letters will still be visible and that's the best you can do.

The answer is (A).

End of Section

Points and Space Tips

<u>What is the longest distance between two points?</u>

The pythagorean theorem works in 3D. So if you are going from one point to another in a cube or rectangular prism, the distance is the square root of the sum of the squares of THREE numbers.

For a cube (side = a) the corner to far corner distance is $d^2 = 3a^2$.

Here's another good one: On a cube with edge a, what's the distance from the center of the front face to a corner of the back face?
Answer: $d^2 = a^2 + a^2/4 + a^2/4 = 6a^2/4$.

The shortest distance from a point to a line is the perpendicular.

All the points (an infinite number of them) a certain distance away from another point make a circle.

If the distance from the endpoints of a segment to some point P is the same then P is on the perpendicular bisector of the segment (this is obvious if you draw a diagram).

Between any two points on a line or on an arc of a circle, there are an *infinite* number of points.

If A + B = N then the product AB is largest when A and B are both N/2.

Another good one is if AB = x and B is the bigger one then B is greater than or equal to the square root of x.

Or you could say if AB = x and A and B are different then one of the numbers has to be bigger than the square root of x.

Units

Prices, Percents, 2D, 3D

compound interest, markups/markdowns, rpm's, algebraic percents, surface area, volume, volume unit conversions, scale of maps

Algebra

given algebraic quantities combine to get another quantity, percents, rates, speeds

Prices, Percents, 2D, 3D

1. A politician puts $1,000 into an account at Bank of Anything For You (BOAFY) that earns 50% interest per year. If no withdrawals are made, approximately how much money will be in the account at the end of four years?

When you increase something by 50% you multiply it by 1.5. (If you increase it by 10%, you multiply it by 1.1.)

Anyway, increasing 50% for four years in a row means multiplying by:

$$1.5^4 = (3/2)^4 = 81/16 \approx 5.$$

The answer is 5000 or (B).

2. Another politician makes an initial deposit of $1,000 at BOAFY. Every year the amount of money in the account increases by x percent. No money is withdrawn. After 10 years there is $12,000 in the account. Which equation is correct?

Suppose x is 30. This means you would multiply your original 1000 dollars by 1.3 every year. In terms of x, this is $(1+x/100)$.

Since you increase by x percent for 10 years you multiply the original amount by $(1+x/100)$ ten times which is the same as taking it to the tenth power.

Since you ended up with 12 times the original amount, multiplying by $(1+x/100)$ ten times must be the same as multiplying by 12.

The answer is (E).

<u>Note</u>: Since there are x's in the answers, you pretend x is known when you are thinking about the problem.

3. Joe-the-sucker has \$32 left after playing a gambling game in which you are guaranteed to lose exactly one-third of your money every time you play. Joe played 5 times before he wised up. The first time he played, he played with all the money in his pocket. Each time after the first time, he played with whatever money he had left. How much money did Joe start with?

Losing a third means multiplying by 2/3. (In the same way, decreasing by 10% means multiplying by 0.9).

So $(2/3)^5$ (since he played 5 times) multiplied by the amount of money he started with must be 32.

Since $(2/3)^5 = 32/243$, he must have started with 243 dollars.

The answer is (C).

Note: If he started with x dollars then,

$$\left(\frac{2}{3}\right)^5 \cdot x = \frac{32}{243} \cdot x = 32 \implies x = 243$$

4. An unscrupulous store wants to have a Christmas sale in which everything is marked 20% off. However, they don't want to actually reduce any of their prices. So, early in November, they mark up everything in the store by x percent so that when they take 20% off the day after Thanksgiving, everything will be back to its original price. What is x?

Taking 20% off means multiplying the marked up price by $0.8 = 4/5$.

But first you do a mark up of M which means multiplying the original price (call it P) by M.

If you mark up and then mark down and you are back to the original price then:

$$\frac{4}{5} \cdot M \cdot P = P \implies \frac{4}{5}M = 1 \implies M = \frac{5}{4} = 1.25$$

Multiplying by $M = 1.25$ is a 25% markup.

So $x = 25$ and the answer is (D).

Note: For a hard question at the end of a section, the chances of the answer being the "obvious" one (20%) are pretty much zero.

5. Farmer Brown divided his k acre farm into two parcels, A and B. Parcel A was $\frac{1}{3}k$ acres and he sold x percent of it. He sold y percent of parcel B. What percent of the whole farm was sold?

The fraction of parcel A sold is $x/100$. The number of acres of parcel A sold is the fraction sold times then number of acres in parcel A:

$$\text{Acres sold from parcel A} = \frac{x}{100} \cdot \frac{k}{3}.$$

The fraction of parcel B sold is $y/100$. The number of acres of parcel B sold is the fraction sold times the number of acres in parcel B.

$$\text{Acres sold from parcel B} = \frac{y}{100} \cdot \frac{2k}{3}.$$

To get the percent of the whole farm we need to do the total acres sold divided by the total acres in the farm and then multiply by 100:

$$\text{percent sold} = 100 \left(\frac{\frac{x}{100} \cdot \frac{k}{3} + \frac{y}{100} \cdot \frac{2k}{3}}{k} \right) = \frac{x + 2y}{3}.$$

The answer is (D).

<u>Note</u>: In general, the most useful thing to have is the actual amount of something; the second most useful thing is the fraction; the third most useful thing is the percent.

6. The radius of each of the 4 tires on a car is 30 cm. If the car travels at 72 km per hour, how many revolutions per minute are made by each tire? (1 km=1000 meters; 1 meter=100 cm)

I like to set up the units so that everything that needs to cancel cancels. Then I put in the numbers. Here are the units:

$$\frac{\text{meter}}{\text{hr}} \cdot \frac{\text{rev}}{\text{meter}} \cdot \frac{\text{hr}}{\text{min}} = \frac{\text{rev}}{\text{min}}.$$

Now put in the numbers:

$$72000 \cdot \frac{1}{2\pi(0.3)} \cdot \frac{1}{60} = \frac{2000}{\pi}.$$

The answer is (A).

<u>Note</u>: There is always 1 revolution for every $2\pi r$ meters and 1 hour is always 60 minutes.

7. The inside of a small hollow cube has a total surface area of 24 square centimeters. A larger hollow cube has inside edges that measure 8 centimeters in length. Wanda drills a hole in the top face of each cube. She fills the small cube with water and then pours the water from the small cube into the large cube without spilling. Wanda repeats this process until the large cube is filled with water. How many times (total) does Wanda fill the small cube with water?

Each of the six faces of the small cube has surface area 4 square cm (because the total is 24). This means the small cube is 2x2x2 which makes the volume 8 cubic cm.

The volume of the larger 8x8x8 cube is 8·8·8 cubic cm, therefore:

$$\frac{\text{Large}}{\text{Small}} = \frac{8 \cdot 8 \cdot 8}{8} = 64.$$

So Wanda fills the small cube 64 times (C).

8! The sum of the lengths of all the edges of a cube is equal to p cm. The surface area of the cube is equal to a square cm. Which of the following must be FALSE?

This is a classic "relate two variables via a third variable" problem. In this case, the crucial third variable is s, the length of one side (or edge) of the cube.

A cube has 12 edges so $p = 12s$.

A cube has 6 faces so $a = 6s^2$.

All of the answers except (C) have different powers of s on each side of the equation, so they can all be solved for s.

Let's see what choice (C) would lead to:

$$a = p^2 \implies 6s^2 = 144s^2 \implies 6 = 144.$$

BZZZZZT!!!

There is no s that will make (C) true (except zero but then there would be no cube) so the answer is (C).

<u>Note</u>: What makes questions like this hard is that you don't get a lot of problems in textbooks that have no solutions (systems of equations yes but actual problems no). Most people aren't used to seeing equations like $6s^2 = 144s^2$ so they don't know how to interpret it and they get the problem wrong. SATAN does this on purpose.

9. A one liter can of paint is used by the legendary Peter the Perfect Painter to perfectly cover exactly 100 square feet of non-porous wall perfectly evenly. All the paint is used. Approximately how thick in <u>millimeters</u> is the layer of paint?
(1 liter = 1000 cubic centimeters; 1 inch = 2.5 centimeters (approx.); 1 centimeter = 10 millimeters)

You might as well assume the wall is 10 feet by 10 feet. This means it is 120 inches by 120 inches or 300 cm by 300 cm (120 times 2.5 is 300).

So the wall is 300 times 300 equals 90,000 square cm in area and is covered by 1000 cubic cm of paint from the 1 liter can. Therefore:

$$90,000 \text{ cm}^2 \cdot \text{thickness in cm} = 1000 \text{ cm}^3$$

The thickness of the layer of paint is 1/90 of a cm.

Now we convert carefully:

$$\frac{1}{90} \text{ cm} \cdot \frac{10\text{mm}}{1\text{cm}} = \frac{1}{9} \text{ mm}$$

It said "approximately" so the answer is 0.1 or (A).

<u>Note</u>: The exact answer is 0.111 repeating. On the fill in section of the test you'd put .111. They would actually mark .11 wrong because .111 is slightly more accurate.

10. A right circular cylinder has a lateral area of a square inches and a volume of v cubic inches. If $a = v = x$, what is the value of x?

We'll set the lateral area equal to the volume and see what happens:

$$2\pi r h = \pi r^2 h \implies r = 2.$$

That's nice, the h cancels and we've figured out that if the lateral area is numerically equal to the volume of a cylinder then the radius must be 2 no matter what h is.

However, h could be anything so there is no way to get the actual lateral area or the actual volume.

The answer is (E).

End of Section

_____

Prices, Percents, 2D, 3D Tips

<u>What would the SAT cost if it were discounted 5% a year for 30 years?</u>

To reduce by 30 percent don't get 30 percent and then subtract, just multiply by 0.7.

To increase by 30 percent, don't get 30 percent and then add, just multiply by 1.3.

If you can, first get the actual number (of whatever), then get the fraction by dividing by the total, then get the percent by multiplying by 100.

If you are given a percent, convert it to a fraction by dividing by 100.

$2\pi R$ is meters per revolution.

$1/2\pi R$ is revolutions per meter.

Set up the units so you get the right cancellations, then put in the numbers.

There are 144 square inches in a square foot, NOT 12.

If you have two variables that are equal, look for a third variable that is related to your original two.

Algebra

1. It takes G gallons of water to fill 6 hot-tubs. If you have N gallons of water but use 80% of it to water the lawn, how many hot-tubs can you fill using the remaining water?

It's 6/G hot-tubs per gallon and N/5 gallons (4/5 was used to water the lawn). Here are the units:

$$\frac{\text{tubs}}{\text{gallons}} \cdot \text{gallons} = \text{tubs} \quad .$$

Now you can replace the units with numbers and/or variables:

$$\frac{6}{G} \cdot \frac{N}{5} = \frac{6N}{5G} .$$

So the answer is (A).

Note: Any given info such as gallons per tub can be turned upside down if it is convenient.

2. Joe (an SAT connoisseur) decides chocolate covered cockroaches would go well with the test so he plans to sneak some in for his 8th attempt at a 2400. He can buy n cockroaches for d dollars. The price per cockroach is independent of the number of roaches purchased. How much will it cost in dollars for Joe to buy n^3 chocolate covered cockroaches?

First set up the units:

$$\frac{\text{dollars}}{\text{roach}} \cdot \text{roaches} = \text{dollars} \quad .$$

Then put in the letters:

$$\frac{d}{n} \cdot n^3 = dn^2 \quad .$$

So the answer is (C).

3. Hoping to miss her scheduled SAT at the PainIsGood test center, Lily drives one third of the distance to the test center at 30 miles per hour (mph), one third of the distance at 20 mph, and the final third at 15 mph. She does annoy the other drivers but does not miss the test. What is Lily's average speed for her agonizing trip to the test center?

This is a classic trick. You DON'T average the three speeds. The answer is NOT $65/3 = 21.67$ mph.

The actual answer is less than this because Lily spends more time driving at 15 mph than she does at the faster speeds.

To get the average speed, you have to do total distance over total time.

Let's say each of her three legs is a distance equal to x. That would make the total distance equal to $3x$. To get the total time you have to add up the times for each leg. For example, the fast leg takes $x/30$ hours (because miles over miles per hour equals hours).

Here's the whole calculation:

$$\text{avg speed} = \frac{\text{distance}}{\text{time}} = \frac{3x}{\frac{x}{30} + \frac{x}{20} + \frac{x}{15}} = \frac{3x}{\frac{9x}{60}} = 20.$$

So it just happens to be one of the speeds, 20 mph, or (C).

4. One Super Lube Dude can do x oil changes per year. The lovely town of Carsville has y cars. If all oil changes are performed at Super Lube and all cars get exactly 3 oil changes per year, how many Super Lube Dudes are needed to take care of all the cars in Carsville?

The trick, with "per year" problems is to assume you are talking about 1 year. You are given:

$$\frac{1 \text{ Dude}}{x \text{ oil changes}}$$

and

$$\frac{3 \text{ oil changes}}{1 \text{ car}}$$

and

y cars.

If you multiply everything, "oil changes" cancels, "car(s)" cancels, and you get $3y/x$ "dudes" (B).

Note: "Cars" and "Car" are the same thing so they cancel. It wasn't necessary to turn anything upside down for this one.

5. Every time a question is answered incorrectly or left blank by someone taking the SAT, SATAN laughs with delight and Hell gets hotter. The rate of temperature increase in Hell is d degrees for every x questions NOT answered correctly. One year, N people took the SAT and the average test-taker answered p percent of Q questions correctly. By how many degrees did Hell get hotter that year due to the SAT?

Working backwards we know the fraction of questions answered correctly is $p/100$ (always convert percents to fractions). The fraction not answered correctly is $1 - p/100$.

Multiply the fraction by Q to get the number not answered correctly by the average test-taker and multiply that by N to get the total number of questions not answered correctly.

The result is:

$$NQ \cdot (1 - p/100).$$

Since Hell gets hotter by d/x degrees per question not answered correctly, you multiply d/x by the expression above to get the answer (A).

6. In Piano City, there are n pianos that are each tuned exactly once a year. There are t piano tuners in the city. A tuner is paid d dollars for every 5 pianos tuned. What is the average income in dollars per year earned by a tuner for tuning pianos in Piano City?

Another "per year" problem so assume 1 year. You've got n pianos per city, t tuners per city, and $d/5$ dollars per piano.

We want to get dollars per tuner. "Pianos" and "city" must cancel. First do the units:

$$\frac{\text{dollars}}{\text{piano}} \cdot \frac{\text{pianos}}{\text{city}} \cdot \frac{\text{city}}{\text{tuners}} = \frac{\text{dollars}}{\text{tuner}}.$$

Now substitute using the given information:

$$\frac{d}{5} \cdot n \cdot \frac{1}{t} = \frac{dn}{5t}.$$

So the answer is (C).

<u>Note</u>: We had to turn tuners per city upside down.

7. A bicycle has two wheels each with radius r meters. Ryder rides the bicycle five times around a circular track with radius R meters. How many rotations are made by each wheel?

The total distance Ryder rides is 5 times $2\pi R = 10\pi R$ meters (since he goes around the track 5 times).

Each wheel has to rotate $10\pi R$ meters and we want to know how many rotations that is (the number of wheels doesn't matter).

We have meters but we need rotations. So we multiply by rotations/meters.

We know that 1 rotation of the bicycle wheel is $2\pi r$ meters.

Here are the units and variables all together:

$$10\pi R \text{ meters} \cdot \frac{1 \text{ rotation}}{2\pi r \text{ meters}} = \frac{5R}{r} \text{ rotations}.$$

The answer is (B).

Questions 8-10: Some college students who have trouble adjusting to "daily life without mommy" respond by drinking alcohol until they vomit. The technical term used by mental health professionals to refer to this behavior is "stupid." The technical term for people who drink <u>more than</u> six ounces of liquor <u>per hour</u> at a party is "moronic." People who are moronic are not considered stupid (they are beyond stupid) although they may vomit.

8. There were x moronic people at a party out of a total of N people. Thirty percent of the people who were not moronic were stupid. What percent of the people at the party were stupid?

To get the percent of people who were stupid, the simplest method is to get the *number* of people who were stupid, divide that by N to get the *fraction* of people who were stupid, and then multiply by 100 to get the *percent* stupid.

The number of people at the party who were not moronic is $N-x$. So the *number* of stupid people is $0.3(N-x)$.

Divide by N to get that the *fraction* of stupid people is $0.3(1-x/N)$.

Multiply by 100 to get that the *percent* of stupid people is $30(1-x/N)$.

The answer is (A).

Questions 8-10: Some college students who have trouble adjusting to "daily life without mommy" respond by drinking alcohol until they vomit. The technical term used by mental health professionals to refer to this behavior is "stupid." The technical term for people who drink <u>more than</u> six ounces of liquor <u>per hour</u> at a party is "moronic." People who are moronic are not considered stupid (they are beyond stupid) although they may vomit.

9. At a party, there were x stupid people and y moronic people and $x + y = 72$. All 72 vomited and 20 of them lost consciousness (passed out). The number of unconscious morons was 4 times the number of unconscious stupid people. Ten percent of stupid people passed out. What percent of moronic people passed out?

The 20 unconscious people were divided 4 to 1 (morons : stupids). That means there were 16 unconscious morons and 4 unconscious stupids.

The 4 stupids are 10 percent of the total stupids, so there were 40 stupid people. That leaves 32 moronic people (the total was given as 72). Since 16 morons out of 32 passed out, the answer is 50 percent (B).

<u>Note</u>: A quick way to divide 20 into 4 to 1 is to think "5 parts" with each "part" equal to 4.

10. At a party with N people, there were no moronic people. One third of the people at this party didn't drink any alcohol. There were x bottles of hard liquor at the party each containing y ounces of liquor. If the party lasted 3 hours, what is the maximum number of bottles that could have been consumed at the party?

To get the largest possible liquor consumption, assume two-thirds of the people ($2N/3$) drink 6 ounces per hour each (the most they can drink without being morons).

So the $2N/3$ people each drink 18 ounces for the whole three-hour party. Each bottle has y ounces. We want people and ounces to cancel and we want to be left with bottles. Therefore:

$$\frac{2N}{3} \text{ people} \cdot \frac{18 \text{ ounces}}{\text{person}} \cdot \frac{1 \text{ bottle}}{y \text{ ounces}} = \frac{12N}{y} \text{ bottles}$$

The answer is (B).

<u>Note</u>: The value of x is irrelevant here although it must be true that $x \geq 12N/y$. If, on the other hand, $x < 12N/y$ then the answer to the question would be x.

End of Section

_____

Units Algebra Tips

<u>Cockroaches, vomiting, and the fires of Hell. So sorry.</u>

If 6 maggots fit in your nose you can choose either 6 maggots/nose or 1/6 nose/maggot. You might call this the upside-down rule.

Figure out what unit you're looking for and then set up the units so they cancel everything but the thing you want.

Don't worry about plurals: "maggots" and "maggot" are the same unit.

If you want something on top but it's on the bottom just turn it upside-down.

Don't think too much: set up and solve.

The <u>number</u> of idiots employed by STS is the <u>fraction</u> of idiots times the <u>total</u> number of employees.

The <u>percent</u> of idiots is the <u>fraction</u> of idiots times 100.

The <u>fraction</u> of idiots is the <u>percent</u> of idiots divided by 100.

Statistics

Warmup

mean, median, mode basic definitions (not SAT-like)

Averages

changes in average, possible values given average, algebra problems involving averages, average of a combined group, average as a constraint

Probability

get P given ratios, get P given numbers, express P in terms of x, dual probabilities, get P from counting, applications of P (statistical surveys and studies)

Mean, Median, Mode

comparison of mean and median, possibilities given constraints, algebraic word problems based on MMM, effect of changes to set on MMM of the set

Warmup

1. The median of 10, 10, 10, 10, 10 is:

It's just 10. You write down the numbers in order and pick the one in the physical middle. If you have an even number of numbers, you take the average of the numbers on either side of the physical middle.

The answer is (C).

2. The median of 2, 8, 8, 12 is:

The physical middle is between 8 and 8 and the average of 8 and 8 is 8.

The answer is (B).

3. The median of 2, 2, 3, 7, 9 is:

The physical middle is 3.

The answer is (B).

4. The median of 2, 2, 3, 100 is:

The physical middle is between 2 and 3 and the average of 2 and 3 is 2.5.

The answer is (E).

5. The median of 2, 2, 2, 6 is:

The physical middle is between 2 and 2 so the median is 2.

The answer is (A).

6. The mode of 2, 8, 8, 12 is:

The mode is the most common number, in this case 8.

The answer is (B).

7. The mode of 2, 5, 9, 11 is:

If there are ties, you have multiple modes.

In this case, the answer is (E).

_____

8. The mode of 2, 2, 8, 8, 10 is:

You can have more than one mode if there is a tie so 2 and 8 are both modes.

The answer is (D).

9. The median of 1, 2, 3, 50, 50, 70, 80 is:

The physical middle is the first 50 so the median is 50.

The answer is (C).

_____

10. Which of the following is true of the set of four numbers a, b, c, d?

Just because they have different letters doesn't mean the numbers are different. And just because the letters are in order doesn't mean the numbers they represent are in order. It could be 1, 1, 1, 1 or 1, 2, 3, 4, or 4, 3, 2, 1 or 1, 657, 9, 0. You don't know. If they don't say, make no assumptions.

The answer is (E).

End of Section

_____

Averages

1. In a typical day at the TSA (Testing School of America), Sally takes five tests. Her score on the first test is x. On each test after the first, her score is 4 points lower than her score on the previous test. What is her average score for all five tests?

Her test scores are x, $x–4$, $x–8$, $x–12$, and $x–16$. The total is $5x–40$ so the average is $x–8$.

$$\text{average} = \frac{\text{sum of tests}}{\text{number of tests}} = \frac{5x - 40}{5} = x - 8.$$

The answer is (A).

2. Sally is scheduled to take her Nth test at the TSA. She has an average of A for her first $N–1$ tests. She is finally fed up and doesn't bother to show up for the Nth test. She receives a zero for this test. How many points lower than A is Sally's average for all N tests?

Sally lost A points as a result of the zero on the last test. This loss is divided evenly among all N tests so her new average is A/N less than the old average.

The answer is (A).

Note 1: Since Sally averaged A on N-1 tests, her total must have been $A \cdot (N$-1$)$. You can divide this by N to get Sally's average after her zero.

$$\text{new average} = \frac{A \cdot (N - 1)}{N} = A - \frac{A}{N}$$

This is another way to see that her average dropped by A/N.

Note 2: What is the average of 95, 91, 88, 86? Here's a shortcut. The second test is a loss of 4 points (relative to the 95), the third test is a loss of 7 points, and the fourth test is a loss of 9 points. Your total loss is 20 points. Dividing this loss among 4 tests, you get a loss of 5 points (relative to 95). So the average is 90.

3. The average of four positive numbers is 70. Which of the following is true?

    I.   If one number is 60, one number must be 80.

    II.   At least one number is greater than 70.

    III. The largest number cannot be 300.

All you know about these numbers is that they are all positive and they add up to 280 (an average is SATAN's way of telling you the sum).

You could have 60, 70, 71 and 79 for instance so I is NOT true.

You could have 70, 70, 70, and 70 so II is NOT true.

Since all the numbers are positive, you can't have 300 and have them add to 280 so III is true and the answer is (D).

4. The average of five positive integers is 50. One of the five integers is 26. The largest possible value of one of the other four numbers is:

Five numbers with an average of 50 must add up to 250. To make one of them as big as possible, you could make four of them 26, 1, 1, 1 (if they were five *different* positive integers you would make them 26, 1, 2, 3).

If your first four numbers are 26, 1, 1, and 1, the other number must be 221 so that they add up to 250.

The answer is (D).

5. The average of a, b, c, and d is equal to y and the value of d is 12 less than the value of y. The average of a, b, and c must be:

Here's the quick way. If d is 12 *less* than the average then the other three numbers have to (collectively) make up the difference. If they were each 4 *more* than the average then that would balance out the little guy (d). So the average of a, b, and c has to be $y+4$ and the answer is (D).

Or you can just do it by brute force. We are given that,

$$\frac{a+b+c+d}{4} = y \text{ and } d = y - 12.$$

A little substituting and rearranging and you get:

$$a+b+c = 3y+12 \implies \frac{a+b+c}{3} = y+4.$$

Again, the answer is (D).

Note: Suppose you get an 80 on the first of four tests. What scores do you need on the remaining three tests to end up with an average of 92? You need to gain 12 points above 92. So three 96's or an average of 96 would do it.

6. One group of people (group I) has an average height of 62 inches. Another group (group II) has an average height of 70 inches. The average height of <u>all</u> the people in both groups together is 67 inches. If there are 120 people in group I, how many are in group II?

You may not want to be too clever with this one but there are obviously more people in group II because the overall average only 3 away from the group II average but 5 away from the group I average. The super quick way is to multiply 120 by 5/3 to get 200.

A safer method is to assume there are N people in group II and write down this equation:

$$120 \cdot 62 + N \cdot 70 = (120+N) \cdot 67.$$

The total height of group I plus the total height of group II equals the total height of the combined group.

If you solve for N you get 200 (E).

7. Jack is an independent contractor working for a radioactive isotope production company. Jack earns 30 dollars per hour for routine checks and 45 dollars per hour for work in radioactive areas. On one particular day he earns d dollars for routine checks and another d dollars for work in a radioactive area. He doesn't take any breaks. What is the average number of dollars per hour (dollars earned divided by hours worked) Jack earns that day?

If you think about this one, you'll get it wrong.

The trick is to calculate dollars earned over hours worked mechanically.

Jack worked for $d/30$ (dollars over dollars per hour) hours on routine checks and $d/45$ hours in radioactive areas. In this time $(d/30 + d/45)$ he earned $2d$ dollars.

Divide total dollars earned by total hours worked to get the average number of dollars per hour:

$$\frac{2d}{\frac{d}{30}+\frac{d}{45}} = \frac{2}{\frac{1}{30}+\frac{1}{45}} = \frac{2}{\frac{5}{90}} = 36$$

The reason his average rate is closer to his rate for routine checks is that he spent longer doing the routine checks than he did in the radioactive area.

The answer is (B).

8. The average of a and b is x. The average of a, b, c, and d is $1.5b$. If $a/b = 3$, what is the average of c and d?

Remember, the average gives you the sum so we have these equations:

$a + b = 2x$,
$a + b + c + d = 6b$ and
$a = 3b$.

and we're looking for the sum of c and d.

All of the answers have an x so we have to boil everything down to only x's. The main thing to get is:

$3b + b = 2x \implies b = x/2$.

Now substitute into the second equation above and get:

$2x + c + d = 6b = 3x \implies c + d = x$.

So the average of c and d is $x/2$ or (B).

9. The set of different integers a, b, c, and d has an average equal to x. The average of a^2, b^2, c^2, and d^2 is equal to y. Which of the following statements must be true?

   I. $y > 2$

   II. $y = x^2$

   III. $y > x$

To check I, try to falsify it: in other words, try to make y less than or equal to 2. The smallest possible y is obtained by using $(-1, 0, 1, 2)$ as your four integers. In this case, the average of the squares is $y = 6/4 = 1.5$. So I is not true.

The average of the squares is not the same as the square of the average. Checking it with 0, 1, 2, and 3 ($x=1.5$, $x^2=2.25$, $y=3.5$) will verify that II is not true.

Two of the integers could be 0 and 1 which do not increase when squared. But the other two integers would have to increase when squared so III must be true.

The answer is (D).

<u>Note</u>: It's important on the SAT to remember that integers can be negative. If you picked 0, 1, 2, and 3 as your smallest set, you would get 3.5 as your smallest average and draw the wrong conclusion.

10! The average of 5 different integers is 20. The largest of the 5 integers is 23. The smallest of the five integers is N. How many possible values of N are there?

First find out how low N can go. Obviously the biggest first four are 23, 22, 21, and 20. So we are a total of $3+2+1 = 6$ over 20. That means N has to be 6 less than 20 which is 14.

So we start with 23, 22, 21, 20, 14 as our "basic group" of 5 numbers with an average of 20 and a largest value of 23.

Can N be 15 (one more than 14)? Sure. Just turn the 20 in the basic group into a 19.

How about 16? No problem, just turn the 20 in the basic group into an 18 (or turn the 21 into a 19).

Can the smallest number be 17? This is easy, just turn the 22 into a 19.

And now we try 18. Turning the 22 into a 19 won't work because 18, 19, 20, 21, 23 has an average above 20. You can't change the 23 so you're stuck — 18 just won't work.

So there are 4 possibilities for the smallest number N: 14, 15, 16, and 17 and the answer is (B).

End of Section

Averages Tips

<u>You're a mean one, Mr. Grinch.</u>

An average is often just a way to tell you the sum. If the average of 4 numbers is x, their sum is $4x$.

The sum is often more useful to you than the average.

If you get 95, 95, 95, 95, and 90 on tests, you "lost" 5 points on the last test which works out to 1 point on your average of all 5 tests. The average is 94.

Average and "mean" are the same thing.

If you get an 80 on one test, you must average 92.5 on the next four to have an average of 90 for all five tests. It's a matter of making up 10 points.

If you drive 30 miles at 30 mph and then drive another 30 miles at 60 mph, your average speed is 40 mph = 60 miles/1.5 hrs NOT the average of 30 mph and 60 mph. (This happens because you went at the slower speed for a longer time.)

If you have 5 numbers whose average is 50 and the first four are 45, 47, 49, and 50, the last number is 50+5+3+1 = 59. This is a good trick.

Probability

1. A bag has blue, green, and yellow marbles. There are 3 times as many green marbles as yellow marbles and 4 times as many blue marbles as green marbles. What is the probability of randomly selecting a yellow marble?

As usual with "3 times as many" type problems, you say the smallest one is x and the other one is $3x$.

So we have x yellow marbles, $3x$ green marbles, $12x$ blue marbles and $16x$ total marbles (it's important to have the totals when you are doing probability).

$$P_{yellow} = \frac{\text{number of yellow}}{\text{total marbles}} = \frac{x}{16x} = \frac{1}{16}.$$

The answer is (A).

Note: If you assume 1 yellow marble, there would be 3 green marbles, 12 blue marbles, and 16 marbles total. Again, the probability of picking yellow is $1/16$.

2. A bag contains N marbles. A marble selected at random from the bag could be one of m different colors. There are x ($x > 1$) marbles of each color in the bag. What is the minimum number of marbles you must select at random from the bag in order to be 100% certain you will have (outside the bag) a pair of marbles of the same color?

Suppose there are 18 marbles with colors red, green, or blue and 6 of each color. (Picking definite numbers is often useful.)

You want either 2 reds, 2 blues, or 2 greens. You go to pick marbles and you are very unlucky. You pick a red, then a green, then a blue. No pair yet. On your fourth pick, you are guaranteed a pair.

So the answer is $m+1$ or (B).

Note: For this problem, no calculation was necessary, just careful reading, a concrete picture, and common sense. Watch for those.

3. Another blue, green, and yellow marble bag. The probability of picking a blue marble is 1/2. The probability of picking a green marble is 1/3. There are twenty yellow marbles in the bag. Which of the following is true about this bag of marbles?

    I.   There are 40 blue marbles.

    II.   There are 30 green marbles.

    III.   The probability of picking a yellow marble is 1/5.

The total probability is always 1. We can use this to find the probability of picking a yellow marble:

$$P_{\text{yellow}} = 1 - \tfrac{1}{2} - \tfrac{1}{3} = \tfrac{1}{6}.$$

Since there are twenty yellows, there are $6 \cdot 20 = 120$ marbles total.

That means there's $(1/2) \cdot 120 = 60$ blue marbles and $(1/3) \cdot 120 = 40$ green marbles.

So none of the possibilities (I, II, or III) is true and the answer is (A).

4. Yet another bag. Same colors. There are twice as many green marbles as yellow marbles. The probability of picking a blue marble is 4/5. The number of green marbles is x. What is the number of blue marbles?

Since blue is 4/5 that means green and yellow put together is 1/5. Since there are twice as many greens as yellow, green must be 2/15 and yellow 1/15.

Note that "twice as many" means "divide into three parts." In this case, we have to divide 1/5 into three parts — with each part 1/15.

The probability of picking blue is $4/5 = 12/15$ which is 6 times the probability of picking green.

The answer is (D).

<u>Note</u>: If you assume 1 yellow marble, you would have 2 green marbles. Since 4/5 of the marbles are blue and 1/5 are other colors, there are 4 times as many blue marbles as other marbles. So there would be $4 \cdot 3 = 12$ blue marbles. Again, with this example, you get 6 times as many blue marbles as green marbles.

5. The evil blue, green, and yellow marble bag has an equal number of blue and green marbles. There are four times as many yellow marbles as blue marbles. Some marbles are solid and some are hollow. For each color, there are five times as many solid marbles as hollow marbles. What is the probability of randomly choosing a solid green marble?

You can say there are x blue marbles, x green marbles, $4x$ yellow marbles, and $6x$ total marbles. The probability of picking green is $1/6$.

Since solid is 5 times hollow, the probability of picking solid is $5/6$ and the probability of picking hollow is $1/6$.

So $1/6$ of the marbles are green and $5/6$ of those or $5/36$ are green and solid. The answer is (B).

Note 1: Another way to look at this is the multiplication rule: to get the probability of two things happening, you multiply the individual probabilities:

$$P_{\text{green and solid}} = P_{\text{green}} \cdot P_{\text{solid}} = \frac{1}{6} \cdot \frac{5}{6} = \frac{5}{36} \ .$$

Note 2: If you have 1 hollow green marble, you would have 5 solid green marbles, 1 hollow blue marble, 5 solid blue marbles, 4 hollow yellow marbles, 20 solid yellow marbles, and 36 marbles total. Again, the probability of picking a solid green marble is $5/36$.

6. A slightly more interesting bag with blue, green, and yellow marbles has some marbles that explode when removed from the bag. Only blue marbles explode. There are 162 blue marbles in the bag, not all of which explode. Two-thirds of the marbles in the bag are blue. If one marble is chosen at random from the full bag, the probability that it will explode is $1/9$. What is the ratio of exploding blue marbles to all blue marbles?

We need to figure out how many marbles are in the bag so that we can figure out how many explode.

Since 162 marbles is $2/3$ of the bag there must be $162 \cdot (3/2) = 243$ marbles in the bag.

Of the 243, $1/9$ or 27 of them are exploding blue marbles.

So the ratio of exploding blue marbles to all blue marbles is $27/162 = 1/6$.

The answer is (D).

Note: This one can also be done by multiplication of probabilities:

$$P_{\text{explode}} = P_{\text{blue}} \cdot P_{\text{explode if blue}}$$

or, with numbers:

$$\frac{1}{9} = \frac{2}{3} \cdot \frac{1}{6} \ .$$

7. If the probability of picking a yellow marble out of a bag is $1/n$ and n is an integer greater than 1, what is the ratio of the number of yellow marbles in the bag to the number of other marbles?

Don't waste time thinking about it. Pick a concrete number for n like 5.

In our concrete example, the probability of picking a yellow marble is $1/5$ which means there could be 1 yellow marble and 4 other marbles (or, *e.g.*, 2 yellow marbles and 8 other marbles).

So the ratio of yellow to other is 1 to 4 which is $1/(n\text{-}1)$.

The answer is (D).

8. All of the numbers from 1 to 100 inclusive are written in a single line. If you choose a digit at random from the line of digits, what is the probability that you would choose a 1?

If you can get an answer without being too clever, that's a good thing. Write down all the numbers with a 1:

1, 10, 11, 12, 13, 14, 15, 16, 17, 18, 19, 21, 31, 41, 51, 61, 71, 81, 91, 100.

It's worth it to take a few extra seconds and actually write them all down. Now just count like you're an idiot. You get 21 one's.

There are 9 one-digit numbers and 1 three-digit number so there must be 90 two-digit numbers ($9+1+90 =100$ so that's all of them).

Anyway the total number of digits is $9+3+180 =192$ and $21/192$ reduces to $7/64$.

The answer is (E).

9. A randomly-selected group of people were asked the following question: "Do you think the average high school principal could run a successful business?" The results were as follows: 240 people said NO; 100 people said MAYBE; 20 people said YES. Based on this survey, if you asked another 90 randomly-selected people the same question, how many people would be expected to say NO?

With surveys you assume that the fraction of people who said NO the first time will also be the fraction of people who say NO the second time.

The total number of people surveyed the first time was 360, and 240 out of 360 or 2/3 said NO.

Out of 90 people in the second survey, you would expect 2/3 to say NO.

So the answer is 2/3 of 90 which is 60.

The answer is (B).

10. According to one study, the probability that an American adult ate too much sugar as a child is 80%. According to a companion study, 30% of people who ate too much sugar as children have trouble controlling their weight as adults while only 10% of people who did not eat too much sugar as children have a weight control problem. According to both studies, how many American adults out of 100 would be expected to have trouble controlling their weight?

Out of 100 children, 80 ate too much sugar and 20 did not.

Of the 80 that ate too much sugar, 30%, or 24, will have trouble with their weight.

Out of the 20 who were a bit more health-conscious as kids, 10%, or 2, will have trouble controlling their weight anyway (life is so unfair).

So 24 + 2 = 26 and the answer is (D).

End of Section

Probability Tips

<u>What is the probability that you will get an 800?</u>

Probability is usually a fraction or decimal between 0 and 1.

You can express probability as a percent: 0.3 is 30%.

The probability of getting something good is the number of good things divided by the total number of things.

Since probability is a ratio, you don't need the actual numbers: $3x$ good things divided by $4x$ total things will do just fine.

The total probability is always 1.

Twice as many means two parts out of three compared to one part out of three. Five times as many means 5/6 to 1/6.

The probability of two things being true is the product of their individual probabilities. So if you can do something 7 out of 10 times that means you can do it twice in a row 49 out of 100 times.

It is often easier to work with definite numbers; you can make them up to fit the problem.

If you can do something the stupid, simple way, do it because it's usually safer.

Always get the total if you can.

Percentages are easy to do in your head. For example, 30% of 50 has to be 15 because 3 times 5 is 15 and you know it isn't 1.5 or 150.

Mean, Median, Mode

1. A set of four numbers a, b, c, and d has mean x and median y. Which of the following must be true?

    I. $x \neq y$

    II. $y \neq a$

    III. $x < 4y$

If you have 1, 2, 2, 3 then the mean, median, and mode will all be 2. So I is not always true.

The median can easily be one of the numbers and a, b, c, and d aren't necessarily in order so II is not true.

It's easy to have the mean be way bigger than the median. Take 1, 2, 2, 1000 for instance. So III is not always true either.

The answer is (A).

2! Four positive numbers a, b, c, and d have mean x and median y. If $a<b<c<d$ then which of the following could be true?

    I. $x < y/2$

    II. $y = b$

    III. $x > c$

The median is right in the middle of b and c so:

$$\frac{y}{2} = \frac{(b+c)/2}{2} = \frac{b+c}{4}$$

But $x=(a+b+c+d)/4$ which is definitely bigger than $y/2 = (b+c)/4$. So I is NOT true.

Since b and c are different and the median is between them, II can't be true either.

If you have 1, 2, 3, 1000, the average will be greater than the third number, so III could true and the answer is (C).

Note: This a relatively rare "could be true" question. SATAN usually asks "must be true" questions.

3. A set consists of an odd number of integers with mean *x,* median *y,* and mode *z.* If *z* is a single mode (there are no other numbers with as many multiple occurrences as *z*), then which of the following is always true?

I. *x* is an integer

II. *y* is an integer

III. *z* is an integer

Suppose you have 5 integers. The mean won't be an integer unless the sum happens to be divisible by 5. So I isn't always true.

Since there are an odd number of integers you just pick the physical middle for the median. No averaging is necessary so the median will be an integer. So II is true.

Of course, the mode is one of the numbers so it too is an integer. So III is true and the answer is (C).

4. Three integers *a, b,* and *c* have a median that is two more than the mean. If *a<b<c* and *a=2* and *c=12,* then what is the median?

The median is *b* and the mean is (a+b+c)/3. Also, *a* is 2 and *c* is 12. Since the median (*b*) is two more than the mean we know that:

$$b = \frac{2 + b + 12}{3} + 2.$$

This is easy enough to solve. You get $3b = b+20$ or $b=10$.

The answer is (E).

5. Four numbers a, b, c, and d have a median that is equal to the average. If $a<b<c<d$, then which statement is true?

When the 4 numbers are in order, the median is $(b+c)/2$. The mean is *always* $(a+b+c+d)/4$.

If you set these equal and simplify you get:

$$b+c=a+d$$

which is the same as

$$b-a=d-c.$$

So the answer is (A).

6. A set of N consecutive integers has average A and median M. What is $M-A$?

For any set of consecutive integers the physical middle and the average (or mean) are the same thing.

For example, the median of 1, 2, 3, 4, 5, 6 is 3.5 and so is the average. Using negative numbers in your set doesn't change anything. The mean and median are still equal.

So the answer is (A).

7. The first member of a set of N integers ($N>2$) is 1. Each member of the set after the first is equal to twice the previous member. Which of the following must be true of the set?

I. The mean is greater than the median.

II. The median is an integer.

III. The mean is an integer.

Take 1, 2, 4, 8, 16. Compare it to 1, 2, 4, 6, 7. Both sets have median=4 but only the second set also has mean=4. If the numbers to the right of the median rapidly get bigger, the mean will be "pulled" to the right. So I is true.

The median will either be the middle number or the average of 2 even numbers, so II is true.

The very first mean (from 1, 2, 4) is not an integer so III is NOT true and the answer is (D).

8. Five consecutive positive integers are represented by v, w, x, y, and z in order from smallest to largest. If you replace v with double its value which of the following must be true about the new set of five integers?

I. The mean will be larger than x.

II. The median will be equal to x.

III. The median will be equal to y.

Since the numbers are consecutive, x is the mean as well as the median. If you increase one of the numbers, the mean must increase. So I is true.

Suppose you have 3, 4, 5, 6, 7. If you double the 3, the new median will be 6, so II is not true.

If you have 1, 2, 3, 4, 5, doubling the 1 will not change the median. So III is not true.

The answer is (A).

9. A set contains four numbers. The numbers are represented by x, $4x$, $5x$, and $5x-2$. The set contains three different numbers and one pair of equal numbers. Which of the following is <u>possible</u>?

    I.   The mode is x.

    II.   The mode is $4x$.

    III.   The mode is $5x$.

The one pair of equal numbers gives you the mode.

It could be x because all you have to do is set $5x-2$ equal to x. The same goes for $4x$.

So both I and II are possible.

But you can't have $5x-2$ equal to $5x$. If you tried to solve it for x you would get something crazy like $0=2$ and you would write "no solution."

So III is not possible and the answer is (B).

10. Two of the numbers in a set of 9 positive numbers are changed. As a result of these changes, the median of the set *decreases* and the mean of the set *increases*. Which of the following changes could have this result?

Doubling the highest and halving the second highest (choice A) would increase the mean because you gain more than you lose. If half of the second highest happened to be below the original median, then this change would shift the median down one notch.

So you can just put down your answer, (A).

<u>Note</u>: Choices B, C, and D all increase the mean but they would not decrease the median.

Choice B (doubling the highest and the lowest) keeps the median the same if double the lowest is still below the original median or increases the median if double the lowest is above the original median.

Choice C (doubling the highest and second highest) wouldn't change the median.

Choice D (doubling the highest and halving the lowest) wouldn't change the median either.

End of Section

Mean, Median, Mode Tips

Mean, Meaner, Meanest

Convert equations to words. So *a>b* might translate to "the average is greater than the median."

Use concrete examples to get a "feel" for a problem.

If the number of numbers is odd, the median is always one of the numbers.

If the number of numbers is even, the median may or may not be one of the numbers.

Sometimes algebra is better than using concrete examples. You must make the algebra vs. numbers decision instinctively for each problem.

For consecutive integers, it is always true that mean = median.

The median is the physical middle with the numbers listed in order.

The median often stays put while the mean changes.

Numbers

Divisibility

prime numbers, factors, prime factors, algebraic factors, exponents

Characteristics

positive or negative or fraction, absolute value, odd, even, roots, exponents

Remainders

properties, possible values, applications, modulus, determining from limited information

Digitology

digits in simple math problems, digits in integers, digits in decimals, using bases

Divisibility

1. The integer n is a factor of the integer x and $x > n > 1$. Which of the following must be true?

    I. n is a factor of $x + 15n$

    II. 5 is a factor of $x + 15n$

    III. x is a factor of $x + 15n$

If you divide $x+15n$ by n you get $x/n + 15$. This is an integer because n is a factor of x (x/n is an integer), so I is true.

The other two possibilities are not true because you don't get an integer when you divide.

For II, we don't know that x is divisible by 5.

For III, we don't know that $15n$ is divisible by x.

The answer is (B).

2. The positive integer x is a product of three different prime numbers, p, q, and r. If $r > q > p$, which of the following must be true?

    I.   The greatest prime number that is a factor of x is r.

    II.   If $p > 5$ then x is not divisible by 5.

    III. x^2 is divisible by p, q, and r.

Every number has exactly one prime factorization so p, q, and r are the only prime factors of x. This means I is true.

If the smallest one is bigger than 5, then maybe the prime factors are 7, 11, and 13. However you slice it, 5 isn't on the list so II is true.

Finally, if you square x you get $p \cdot p \cdot q \cdot q \cdot r \cdot r$ which of course is divisible by p, q, and r. So III is true.

The answer is (E).

3! If h, j, and k are prime numbers and $h = 2$ and $x = hjk + 1$ then which of the following is true?

First, x is not divisible by k because you would get hj with remainder 1. So it isn't A.

It can't be B either because we can't be certain that x is divisible by 3. If j or k were 3 then x would not be divisible by 3.

It can't be C because if you get lucky, x might be prime. For example, if $(h, j, k) = (2, 3, 5)$ then x would be 31 which is prime.

On the other hand it can't be D because all we really know about x is that it is not divisible by h, j, or k. If $(h, j, k) = (2, 5, 11)$ then x would be 111 which happens to be divisible by 3.

There is no known formula that always gives prime numbers. If you discover one, you'll be famous.

The answer is (E).

4! If p is a prime number and Q, k, and n are positive integers greater than one and the equation $k^2 n + p^2 = Qkn$ is true, then which of the following must be true?

SATAN loves integer problems with lots of variables because they look like there's not enough information for a solution. This one is slightly harder than a real version but is still excellent practice.

This kind of problem usually involves a prime number like 5. We use p so you can see the general rule. The key is that nothing divides a prime except 1 and itself. So if you know that $p^2/(kn)$ is an integer you know quite a lot.

Imagine dividing the whole equation by kn. Now you can see that $p^2/(kn)$ does indeed have to be an integer. Since k and n can't be 1, they both must be equal to p. Here's the math:

$$\frac{k^2 n + p^2}{kn} = k + \frac{p^2}{kn} = Q \implies kn = p^2 \implies k = n = p.$$

It's really just another way of testing the "primes are only divisible by themselves" rule.

Anyway, the answer is (B).

<u>Note</u>: You can also conclude that $Q = k + 1$.

5. If k and n are positive integers greater than 1 and $n \cdot (k - 6n) = 11$, what is the value of k?

Another great one equation and two unknowns problem that looks like it can't be solved. When SATAN writes questions like this he has a good, long laugh and fire comes out of his ears.

Of course you've got the prime number 11 mixing it up with integers so you can solve the problem even though there's only one equation.

We know that both n and $(k\text{-}6n)$ are integers. The only way to make 11 out of integers is 11 times 1. Since n is given as a "positive integer greater than 1" we know that n must be 11. We have:

$$k - 6n = 1 \text{ and } n = 11 \implies k = 67.$$

The answer is (A).

<u>Note</u>: If you start with integers like k and n, any combination of adding subtracting, and multiplying will leave you with an integer.

6. If j and k are positive integers and $j > k$ and both j and k are divisible by 2, 3, and 5, then the quantity $(j - k)$ must be greater than or equal to:

The smallest value for k is $2\cdot3\cdot5 = 30$.

Since j has to be bigger than k but still have 2, 3, and 5 in it, j must be $2\cdot3\cdot5\cdot x$. The smallest possible x is another 2 so the smallest j is 60 and the smallest difference is 30.

The answer is (B).

7. If j and k are positive integers and $j > k$ and both j and k are divisible by 2, 3, and 8, then the quantity $(j - k)$ must be greater than or equal to:

If you want to be divisible by 2, 3, and 8 all you need are three 2's and one 3. The smallest number that does this is 24.

The next smallest after 24 is 48 (one more 2) and the difference is 24.

So the answer is (C).

Note: The smallest number divisible by 2, 3, and 8 is NOT 2·3·8 because 8 and 2 have a common factor.

8. The quantity 12^{100} is NOT divisible by which of the following?

This huge number is:

$$12^{100} = (2 \cdot 2 \cdot 3)^{100} = 2^{100} \cdot 2^{100} \cdot 3^{100}.$$

It is basically a long string of 2's and 3's.

So if you do $12^{100}/x$, the x will cancel completely as long as it is nothing but 2's and 3's. If there is any other prime number in x, it won't cancel.

The first choice is $18 = 2 \cdot 3 \cdot 3$.

The second choice is $24 = 2 \cdot 2 \cdot 2 \cdot 3$.

The third choice is $27 = 3 \cdot 3 \cdot 3$.

The fourth choice is $30 = 2 \cdot 3 \cdot 5$. The 5 won't cancel so the answer is (D).

The fifth choice is $36 = 2 \cdot 2 \cdot 3 \cdot 3$.

9. If positive integer N is the product of three different prime numbers and if p is the largest prime factor of N, which of the following must be true?

I. $p > \sqrt[3]{N}$

II. $\dfrac{N}{p^2}$ is NOT an integer

III. $\dfrac{N^2}{p}$ is NOT an integer

Let's take a number like 77 which is the product of two primes. Now the square root of 77 is about 8.8. What can you say about the two prime factors? Well, you know for certain that one is above 8.8 and one is below 8.8.

The same reasoning applies to cube roots. With a number like $105 = 3 \cdot 5 \cdot 7$, you are guaranteed that 7 is bigger than the cube root of 105. If it weren't, then $7 \cdot 7 \cdot 7$ would be less than 105!!!

So I is true.

Suppose $N = pqr$ and p, q, and r are prime. If you divide by p once you are left qr. Now qr/p is NOT an integer because the product of two primes is divisible only by the two primes. So II is true.

Since N^2 has two p's in it, there's no problem dividing it by p, so III is NOT true (because it IS an integer) and the answer is (D).

10. If p and n are positive integers and Q is a prime number greater than 3 such that $p^2 - n^2 = 3Q$, then which equation correctly relates the value of Q to the value of n?

If you see a difference of squares on the real SAT, you will often want to factor it especially if it is sitting all alone on one side of the equation. In this case you get:

$(p - n) \cdot (p + n) = 3Q$.

Since $(p - n)$ is a positive integer and $(p + n)$ is also a positive integer and since Q is a prime greater than 3, there is only one way this equation can be true. We must have:

$p - n = 3$ and $p + n = Q$.

Now we can subtract the equations to relate Q to n. We get $2n = Q - 3$. So the answer is (C).

<u>Note 1</u>: A "prime number" is $\{2, 3, 5, 7, 11, \ldots\}$ and is always positive (and usually odd).

<u>Note 2</u>: The answer choices were purposely rigged up so that simple examples for (p, n, Q) like $(4, 1, 5)$ and $(5, 2, 7)$ would be inconclusive.

End of Section

Divisibility Tips

Primal Screams

Primes are to numbers what atoms are to objects.

Primes under 100 are 2, 3, 5, 7, 11, 13, 17, 19, 23, 29, 31, 37, 41, 43, 47, 53, 59, 61, 67, 71, 73, 79, 83, 89, 97.

There are an infinite number of primes and there's no known pattern.

Every number has exactly one set of prime factors (primes that, when multiplied, give the number).

The factors of a number include itself, 1, its prime factors, and every multiplicative combination of its prime factors.

Divisibility means all the prime factors of one cancel with some of the prime factors of the other.

If the digits of a number add up to something divisible by 3 then the original number is divisible by 3. This trick works for 9 also.

If you see a number and you're not sure what to do with it, factor it into its primes and maybe things will suddenly be clear. Remember, in a certain sense, a number IS the product of its primes.

If you divide a number by 5, say, and the remainder is 2, then adding 3 or 8 or 13 to the original number, makes a number divisible by 5. The idea is to create a whole number of extra 5's

If N is divisible by 3 and 5 then it must be divisible by 15. If N is divisible by 9 and 4 then it must be divisible by 36. BUT if N is divisible by 6 and 2 then it may or may not be divisible by 12. The reason: 6 and 2 have a common factor (2).

No matter how many 2's and 3's you have, you'll never make a number divisible by 5 (unless you add them, but that's cheating).

Characteristics

1. If $x^3 < x < x^2$ then

For this kind of problem, there are four types of x's to consider: positive whole numbers, positive fractions, negative fractions, and negative whole numbers.

For positive whole numbers, squaring makes them bigger, and cubing makes them even bigger.

For positive fractions, squaring makes them smaller and cubing even smaller.

For negative fractions, cubing makes them *bigger* because they end up less negative $(-1/2 \to -1/8)$, and squaring makes them even bigger since they become positive.

For negative whole numbers, cubing makes them smaller because they get more negative, and squaring makes them bigger because they become positive.

In this problem, cubing makes it smaller and squaring makes it bigger so it must be a negative whole number (such as –2). So the answer is (D).

2. If $x < x^3 < x^2$ then

This time, cubing makes it bigger and squaring makes it even bigger. So it must be a negative fraction.

The answer is (C).

3! If $x > y$ and $x \neq 0$ and $y \neq 0$ then

If $x = 1$ and $y = -100$, squaring the two numbers will switch the order: y^2 will be bigger. So A is not always true.

With two positive numbers like $x = 10$ and $y = 5$, $1 \backslash x$ will be smaller so B is not always true.

With one positive and one negative like $x = 10$ and $y = -5$, $1/x$ will be bigger so C is not always true.

Cubing a positive and a negative won't change the signs so the original order will be maintained. Even if x and y are fractions, the order won't change when you cube.

The answer is (D).

4! If $x + 2y > 2x - 3y$ then which of the following is true?

I. $\dfrac{x}{y} < 5$

II. The value of x could be greater than the value of y.

III. If $y < 0$ then $x < 0$.

Simplifying the inequality gives you:

$5y > x$ or $x < 5y$.

If y is positive, dividing both sides by y gives:

$\dfrac{x}{y} < 5.$

BUT if y is negative, you get:

$\dfrac{x}{y} > 5.$

Either inequality could be true so (x,y) could be $(2,1)$ OR $(-10,-1)$. So I is not true but II is true.

If $y < 0$ you use the second inequality and x must be negative also since the ratio has to be bigger than $+5$. So III is true.

The answer is (D).

<u>Note</u>: If you divide an inequality by a variable, you get two inequalities corresponding to positive and negative values of the variable. Remember, when you multiply or divide by a negative, the inequality switches direction.

A112

5. If $r < s < t$ ($r \neq 0$, $s \neq 0$, $t \neq 0$) then which of the following must be true?

  I. $rs < st$

  II. $\left| \dfrac{1}{r} \right| > \left| \dfrac{1}{s} \right|$

  III. $s^2 > r$

Since r and s could both be negative with t positive, I doesn't have to be true.

For II, try $r=-100$ and $s=1$. The absolute value of $1/r$ would be very small so II isn't true.

If s is a fraction like $1/3$ and r is a smaller fraction like $1/4$, s squared will be smaller than r. So III isn't true either and the answer is (A).

6. If $y = \left| \dfrac{1}{2-x} \right|$ and $x \neq 2$ then y increases when:

To make y increase you have to make the denominator of the fraction smaller. So you want x to get closer to 2.

Since you are throwing away any negative sign you might get, it doesn't matter if x is above or below 2, just so it gets closer.

With this reasoning, you can see the answer is (C).

7. If a is an integer and $b = a^3$ then which of the following could equal $\sqrt{b}$?

Obviously:

$$(\sqrt{b})^2 = b = a^3$$

so we're looking for a number that, when squared, gives a perfect cube.

The only way this works is if the number is a perfect cube already. That way, when you square it, it will still be a perfect cube.

So 27 has three 3's in it and 27^2 has six 3's and both are perfect cubes.

The answer is (A).

8. If positive integers x and y are both odd and positive integer z is even then which of the following is true?

I. x^z is even

II. $y^z + y^x$ is odd

III. $3 \cdot z^x$ is odd

For I, it doesn't matter how many odd x's you multiply together, there won't be any 2's so it will never become even. So I is not true.

In II, we have the sum of two odd numbers which is always even. So II is not true.

In III, there are plenty of 2's because z has at least one 2. There are at least x 2's in z^x. It only takes one 2 to make a number even so III isn't true either.

The answer is (A).

9. If j and k are integers and $2j + 4 = 4k$ then which of the following must be true?

I. j is even

II. k is even

III. $j \cdot k$ is even

The easiest way is to find a few (j,k) pairs and then check I, II, and III. We'll pick k's and solve for j. Some pairs are: $(-6,-2)$, $(-4, -1)$, $(-2,0)$, $(0,1)$, $(2,2)$.

With examples, you quickly see that k can be any integer but j must be even. So I and III are true.

Another way is to notice that the right side of the equation is divisible by 4 which means the left side must also be divisible by 4. Obviously, 4 is divisible by 4 so the $2j$ must also be divisible by 4 and $2j$ is divisible by 4 only if j is even.

Either way, the answer is (D).

Note 1: Even + even = even. Odd + odd = even. Even + odd = odd. Even times even =even. Even times odd = even. Odd times odd = odd.

Note 2: If you had looked for (j,k) pairs by picking j first, you would have been able to solve for k just fine, but you would get integer values for k only when j was even.

10. If x, y, z, and w are positive integers and $xw + yz + yw + xz$ is odd then which of the following is true?

I.   If x is odd then y is even.

II. $xyzw$ is odd.

III. $(x + w)$ is even.

To make the long sum of 4 products odd, either 1 or 3 of the products have to be odd. For example odd+odd+odd+even = odd or even+even+even+odd = odd.

To test I, assume x and y are both odd. Now there's no way you can get 1 or 3 of the products to be odd. For example, if w is odd and z is even then you'll have odd+even+odd+even = even. So I is true because it can't be false.

The only way II could be true is if x, y, z, and w were all odd but that would give you odd+odd+odd+odd = even. So II is NOT true.

It is possible for $(x+w)$ to be odd. For example, maybe x is odd and w is even. Then if (y, z) is (even, odd), our beautiful sum of four products is: even+even+even+odd = odd. So III is NOT true and the answer is (B).

Note: That was fun but it's quicker to factor the expression to $(x+y)\cdot(z+w)$ = odd and realize that both sums must be odd which means x and y have to be different and z and w have to be different.

End of Section

Characteristics Tips

<u>Numbers are like flowers.</u>

There are 4 basic kinds of numbers. For example: 3, 1/2, -1/3, -6.
You often have to test all four possibilities.

If you divide by a variable in an inequality you get two for the price of one: one has the direction switched and one has the original direction because you don't know if the variable is positive or negative.

Perfect squares: 1, 4, 9, 16, 25, 36, 49, 64, 81, 100, 121, 144, 169, 196, 225, 256, 289, 324, 361, 400.

Perfect Cubes: 1, 8, 27, 64, 125, 216, 343, 512, 729, 1000

Perfect 4th powers: 16, 81, 256, 625

Perfect 5th powers: 32, 243, 1024

A root is either an integer or an irrational number.

If it has one or more 2's, it's even. If it has no 2's, it's odd.

Odd plus Odd is Even.

Even plus Even is Even.

Even plus Odd is Odd.

If you see a quadratic, try to factor it.

$$x^2 - y^2 = (x+y) \cdot (x-y).$$

$$x^2 - 2xy + y^2 = (x-y)^2.$$

$(x+y)^2$ is NOT equal to $x^2 + y^2$.

Remainders

1! If n and k are positive integers greater than 1 and $4kn + 6k + 2$ is divided by $6k$ which of the following could be the remainder?

  I. 1

  II. $4k$

  III. $2k + 2$

There are 3 possible remainders. Let's try a few values of n and look for the pattern we know is there because if there is no pattern in a question like this, SATAN can't ask it.

If $n = 2$, we have $14k + 2$ which has two $6k$'s in it with $2k + 2$ left over as the remainder.

If $n = 3$, we have $18k + 2$ which has exactly three $6k$'s in it. Now all the k's are taken care of and only a 2 is left over.

If $n = 4$, we have $22k + 2$ which has three $6k$'s in it with $4k + 2$ left over as the remainder.

If $n = 5$, we start over again with a $2k$ left over along with the 2 so the remainder is $2k + 2$ again.

So only III is a possible remainder and the answer is (D).

Note: Here's another way. The $6k$ in the middle always divides out, the 2 is always left over, and starting with $n=2$, the first term with $4k$ gives $8k$, $12k$, $16k$, $20k$ . . . *etc.*, which means, after you take out the $6k$'s, the remainders are: $2k$, 0, $4k$, $2k$ . . . *etc.*, plus the 2.

2. The remainder when N is divided by 70 is 58. If today is Monday, what day will it be N days from now?

N has a some unknown number of 70's in it and then there's 58 left over.

Note that 70 days is 10 weeks. So N days is some multiple of 10 weeks plus another 58 days.

Now 58 days is 8 weeks plus 2 days.

So the passage of N days is some multiple of 10 full weeks followed by another 8 full weeks followed by another 2 days.

Of course, it is Monday again after any number of full weeks so after some number of full weeks plus 2 days, it must be Wednesday.

The answer is (C).

3. If n is divided by 90, the remainder is 1. What are the remainders, respectively if $n+179$ and $n+182$ are each divided by 90?

When dividing by 90 (or any number) and looking for remainders, imagine throwing away as many 90's as you can. Whatever is left is your remainder.

With $n+179$, you throw away most of the n and are left with 1+179=180. Since there are exactly two 90's in 180, you can throw it away and you are left with no remainder at all (0).

With $n+182$, you are left with 183 but then you throw away two more 90's and you are left with 3.

The answer is (C).

4. If $n = 5^{50}$ how many different remainders result when n, $n+7$, $n+18$, $n+21$, $n+29$, and $n+32$ are each divided by 11?

You don't know what remainder you get when you divide n or $n+7$ or $n+18$ or $n+whatever$ by 11. What you do know is that if you add a whole number of 11's, the remainder doesn't change.

So $n+7$, $n+18$, and $n+29$ all have the same remainder because they are separated by a whole number of 11's.

Also $n+21$ and $n+32$ have the same remainder. So there are three different remainders. For example if dividing n by 11 gives a remainder of 2, then $n+7$, $n+18$, and $n+29$ will all give a remainder of 9 and $n+21$ and $n+32$ will each give a remainder of 1.

The answer is (A).

5. When positive integer n is divided by 5, the remainder is x. When $2n$ is divided by 5, the remainder is y. Which pair (x, y) is <u>not</u> possible?

The remainder when n is divided by 5 is one member of the set $\{0, 1, 2, 3, 4\}$.

Now you double n, and you get twice as many 5's and you also double the remainder. So your remainders for $2n$ are 0, 2, 4, 6, or 8.

But wait! If the remainder is 6 or 8, you have another 5 and so the remainder is really 1 or 3. The actual set of remainders for $2n$ is $\{0, 2, 4, 1, 3\}$.

So (x, y) could be $(0, 0)$, $(1, 2)$, $(2, 4)$, $(3, 1)$ or $(4, 3)$. Since these are the only possibilities, (x, y) obviously cannot be $(3, 2)$.

The answer is (E).

Questions 6-8: The modulus is defined as follows: $j \bmod k = R$ where R is the remainder when positive integer j is divided by positive integer k.

6. If $j \bmod k = R$ which statement is true for any j and k?

In this problem, you are dividing by k. Suppose you are dividing by 5.

That would mean the remainder R could be 0, 1, 2, 3, or 4. The remainder is always between 0 and one less than the divisor, inclusive.

The answer is (D).

Questions 6-8: The modulus is defined as follows: $j \bmod k = R$

where R is the remainder when positive integer j is divided by positive integer k.

7.   If $j \bmod k = R$ and $j < k$ then

Now you're dividing a small number by a big number. For example, you might be dividing 2 by 13. Obviously there are no 13's in 2 so the answer is 0 with a remainder of 2.

Whenever you divide a small number by a big number, the answer is always 0 with a remainder equal to the small number.

The answer is (A).

8.   If $j \bmod k = R$ and $k < j < 2k$ then

Now your j is at least a decent size. Maybe k is 13 and j is 16 (j would have to be between 13 and 26). If you do 16/13, you get 1 with a remainder of 3. It seems the remainder R is equal to $(j - k)$.

This one example allows you to eliminate A, B, D, and E.

The answer is (C).

9. A positive integer N is divided by 23 and the remainder is 11. What is the remainder if $4N$ is divided by 23?

When you divide N by 23 you throw away a bunch of 23's and you are left with a remainder of 11.

Now you multiply N by 4 and you get 4 times as many 23's. You must also multiply the remainder by 4 so you have a 44 in addition to that big pile of 23's.

Throw away the big pile of 23's AND any extra 23's you got by multiplying the remainder by 4. In this case, there's one extra 23 in the 44 and when you throw it away, you are left with 21.

The answer is (D).

Note: SATAN can also ask: What is the remainder if $N+50$ is divided by 23? Adding 50 gets you two more 23's plus 4 that you have to add to the original remainder. So the remainder when $N+50$ is divided by 23 is 15.

Try this one: What is the remainder if $N+58$ is divided by 23?

10. A positive integer that gives a remainder of 5 when divided by 6 and a remainder of 1 when divided by 3 is called a "6-5-3-1" number. How many 6-5-3-1 numbers below 100 are there?

When you divide some number (call it X) by six and get a remainder of 5 you are saying "there are a bunch of sixes in this number and there's 5 left over."

It doesn't matter how many sixes there are in X. However many there are, you'll have twice as many threes with a 5 still left over. The 5 has one three in it with 2 left over.

So you ALWAYS have twice as many threes as sixes plus one extra and 2 left over. Always.

When you divide our X by three, the remainder is *always* 2.

Here's some math for you masochists out there:

If $X = 6n + 5$ then $X = 3(2n + 1) + 2$.

So there are no "6-5-3-1" numbers and the answer is (A).

Try this one: If you have a number that gives a remainder of 5 when divided by 6, what are the possible remainders if you divide this number by 12?

End of Section

Remainders Tips

What You Never Learned About Remainders

The answer to the "Try this one:" from the solution to #9 is: "zero."

The answer to the "Try this one:" from the solution to #10 is: "5 or 11."

When you divide by 7 the remainder could be 0, 1, 2, 3, 4, 5, or 6. This pattern holds for any number you divide by.

A few simple remainder examples: 13/2 = 6R1; 13/3 = 4R1; 13/5 = 2R3; 13/8 = 1R5; 13/13 = 1R0; 13/14 = 0R13; 13/100 = 0R13.

Add to the remainder: Suppose you divide N by 7 and get a remainder of 4. If you divide N+3 by 7, the remainder is zero because you added 3 to the old remainder and got another 7. If you divide N+6 by 7 your "remainder" is 10 but this 10 contributes another 7 so the actual remainder is 3.

Multiply by the remainder: Suppose you divide N by 7 again and get a remainder of 4. If you multiply N by 6 and divide by 7 again, you get 6 times as many 7's and a remainder of 24 (6 times 4). But the new remainder has three sevens in it so the actual new remainder is 3.

If you are dividing N by 7, then N+5, N+12, N+19 *etc.*, all have the same remainder because you are just adding more 7's. The same is true for N, N+7, and N+14.

If you divide j by k, you might get N with remainder R. This is the same as saying j = Nk+R. In other words, there are N k's in j with R left over.

6 divided by a million is zero with remainder 6: If you divide a small number by a big number you always get 0 with a remainder equal to the small number.

Digitology

AA
+ BB
―――
BBC

1. In the correctly worked addition problem above, A, B, and C represent digits. What digit does C represent?

There is no pair of two digit numbers whose sum is in the 200's. So BB must be 11. Obviously, there is a carry (the carry is 1) — otherwise the result would be CC.

So B is 1 and A+B+1 is 11. This means A is 9. So you are adding 99 and 11 to get 110 and C is 0.

The answer is (A).

AB
+ B
―――
BA

2. In the correctly worked addition problem above, A and B represent digits. What is A?

Obviously there is a carry (with two digits, 1 is the only possible carry) so B has to be 5 or bigger and we have this nice little equation:

$B = A + 1$.

Try all possible B's (5, 6, 7, 8, 9) and see if the nice little equation works.

5 and 5 would mean A=0 which doesn't work. 6, 7, and 8 don't work either. But 9 plus 9 gives you an 8 carry the one and 8 plus 1 is indeed nine.

So B is 9, A is 8. The sum is 89+9=98.

The answer is (D).

3! The sum of 185 consecutive positive integers is equal to N. The units digit of N is equal to u. Assuming the sum can start with any positive integer, how many possible values of u are there?

The units digit of the sum of *any* 180 consecutive integers is always the same.

If you add up the numbers 0 through 9, the result is 45 (units digit is 5). If you add *any* 10 consecutive integers, you're still adding 0 through 9 (not in order) and the units digit is still 5. If you add 18 sets of 10 consecutive integers, you will be adding 18 5's so the units digit will be zero.

But then you're going to add 5 more integers. If the next 5 have units digits 0 through 4, their sum will be 10 and when you add them to your sum, the units digit won't change.

For 1 through 5, the sum is 15 and when you add these 5 to your sum of 180 integers, your units digit will change from zero to 5.

For 2 through 6, the sum is 20. For 3 through 7, the sum is 25. This pattern continues because when you add one to each of 5 integers you add 5 to the sum. The bottom line: the sum of 185 consecutive integers ends in a 5 or a zero.

So the answer is (B).

<u>Note</u>: Going from 5, 6, 7, 8, 9 to 6, 7, 8, 9, 0 you increase by 4 and decrease by 9 and the pattern of zeros and fives continues.

4. If a and b are positive numbers such that $a > b > 0$ and the units digit of the product ab is 2, then which of the following could be the units digit of the difference $a - b$?

The units digit of the product ab is determined by the units digits of a and b. The actual numbers don't matter. For example, the product of 54 and 78 will end with a 2. We don't care about the full number: just knowing that 4 times 8 equals 32 is enough.

There are a total of five pairs of units digits that will get you a 2 as the units digit of the product: (2, 1); (6, 2); (8, 4); (7, 6); and (9, 8).

That is, you can make 2, 12, 32, 42, or 72 out of two digits (multiplied).

When you subtract a and b, you can get any of the following: 1, 9, 4, or 6.

For example, 42 - 26 is 16.

So the answer is (C).

<u>Note</u>: The pair (2,1) gives you 1 or 9 for the difference. The pair (6,2) gives you 4 or 6. The pair (8,4) gives 4 or 6. The pair (7,6) gives 1 or 9 and the pair (9,8) gives 1 or 9.

5! The sum of a two-digit integer x and another two-digit integer y is divisible by 10. The values of the two integers are such that $9<x<y<100$. The integer x may be represented by AB where A is the tens digit of x and B is the units (ones) digit of x. Similarly, y may be represented by CD where C is the tens digit of y and D is the units (ones) digit of y. Which of the following must be true?

I.   If A+B = 8 then D-A = 2.

II. The number of possible values of x is 84.

III. The smallest possible value of y is 20.

If $x + y$ is divisible by 10 then the units digits either add up to 10 or are both zero. If x is 26 then y could be 34, 44, 54, etc., (D has to be 4). Note that D-A does equal 2.

HOWEVER, x could be 80 and y could be 90 which would make I NOT true.

You can't make x 90 because there's no y that has two digits, is greater than x, and ends in zero. You also can't make x, 95, 96, 97, 98, or 99 because there's no y that ends in 5, 4, 3, 2, or 1. So out of the first 99 positive integers you have to leave out 9 (only 1 digit) plus another 6 which means II is true.

You can't have y = 10, 11, 12, 13, 14, or 15 BUT you can have y = 16 and x = 14. So III is NOT true and the answer is (B).

6. The sum of the digits of a four-digit number x is equal to N. Which of the following could be the sum of the digits of $2x$?

I. N

II. $N - 12$

III. $N + 10$

When you double a number you can either increase or decrease the sum of the digits. For example if you double 4000, the sum of the digits goes up by 4. But if you double 5000, the sum of the digits goes *down* by 4.

If you double 5004, the sum of the digits is unchanged so I is true.

If you double 6000, you reduce the sum of the digits from 6 to 3. If you double 6666 you reduce the sum of the digits from 24 to 12 so II is true.

If you double 3331 you increase the sum of the digits from 10 to 20 so III is true.

The answer is (E).

Note: The results of doubling are:

0 --> 0 (no change); 1 --> 2 (change = +1); 2--> 4 (change = +2); 3 --> 6 (change = +3); 4 --> 8 (change = +4); 5 --> 10 (change = –4); 6 --> 12 (change = –3); 7 --> 14 (change = –2); 8 --> 16 (change = –1); 9 --> 18 (no change).

7. If x and y are numbers and A and B represent digits and $\frac{1}{x} = 0.0B$ and $\frac{1}{y} = 0.00A$, what is $\frac{Bx}{Ay}$?

There's nothing fancy here. Remember that 0.03 is 3/100. So 0.0B is $B/100$ and 0.00A is $A/1000$.

$\frac{1}{x} = \frac{B}{100}$ and $\frac{1}{y} = \frac{A}{1000} \implies Bx = 100$ and $Ay = 1000$.

So Bx/Ay is $100/1000 = 1/10 = 0.1$ and the answer is (D).

8. If Q and R are integers and A and B represent digits and $\frac{1}{Q} = 0.0A$ and $\frac{1}{R} = 0.0B$ then one possible value of the product of A and B is:

First replace 0.0A with A/100 and do the same for 0.0B.

Now flip the equations for 1/Q and 1/R upside down to get $Q=100/A$ and $R=100/B$.

Q and R are integers so A and B must go into 100 evenly.

The digits A and B could be 1, 2, 4, or 5 (no other digits go evenly into 100). The product of A and B can't be 6, 12, 15, or 18. But 4 times 5 is 20 so the answer is (E).

Note: On an end-of-section question, SATAN will never say, "A and B are factors of 100, which of these could be their product?" The idea is to write easy questions that are well-disguised and "get" 80% or more of the test takers.

9. In an alphabetic-to-numerical coding system, the single letters A-Z are given values of 0-25 respectively. In a three-letter word, the first letter has value α, the second letter has value β, and the third letter has value γ. The value of a three-letter word is computed as follows:

$$\text{word value} = \alpha \cdot 26^2 + \beta \cdot 26^1 + \gamma \cdot 26^0$$

For example:

$$CAT = 2 \cdot 26^2 + 0 \cdot 26^1 + 19 \cdot 26^0 = 1371$$

What word has the value 783?

Ask yourself "What is the first letter?"

The first letter determines how many "26 squared" you have in the word value. Since 26^2 is 676, you have just one of them in 783. That means the first letter must be B.

The answer has to be (B).

<u>Note</u>: The rest of the 783 comes from the second and third letters. The letter E has a value of 4 and the letter D has a value of 3. Therefore, the value of BED is:

$$1 \cdot 676 + 4 \cdot 26 + 3 \cdot 1 = 783.$$

This is actually a common way to convert words to numbers although in a real system you would use more numbers to accommodate capitals, spaces, punctuation, digits *etc*.

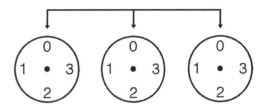

Current Reading: 0 - 0 - 0

10. Each of the three disks shown above rotates clockwise about its center. The disk on the right rotates at the rate of 90° per second. The disk in the middle rotates 90° each time the disk on the right completes one full rotation. The disk on the left rotates 90° each time the disk in the middle completes one full rotation. If the device starts with a reading of 0-0-0, what is its reading after 1 minute has elapsed?

The disk on the right does a complete rotation every 4 seconds. So in 60 seconds it does 15 complete rotations and is back on zero.

The middle disk does 1 click every time the right disk does a complete rotation. That's 15 clicks for the middle disk. Since 4 clicks is a complete rotation, 15 clicks is 3 complete rotations plus 3 clicks. The middle disk lands on 3.

Since the middle disk does three complete rotations, the left disk is on 3. The answer is (E).

End of Section

Digitology Tips

<u>Digits are your friends.</u>

With two digits the carry is either zero or 1.

Don't be afraid of trial and error: ten possibilities isn't that bad.

A number is 100 times the hundreds digits plus 10 times the tens digit plus the ones digit.

Decimals are really fractions in disguise.

A given number (like 48 or 32) doesn't have many factors that are digits and this often limits your possibilities.

It's very helpful on the SAT to know everything about every number below 100. Is it prime? What are its factors? You definitely want to know that 60 is 15 times 4 for example or that 80 is 16 times 5.

When you number starting from zero, object #25 is actually the 26th object.

Many of SATAN's math problems are reading comprehension questions.

Reading

Charts

median, average, interpretation, careful reading, percents, ratios, costs

Charts

Questions 1-3: The graph below shows the correlation between median SAT math score and family income based on (real) data from FairTest.

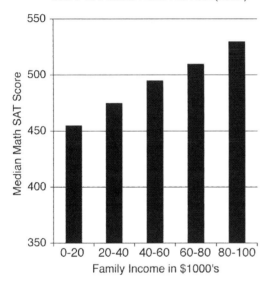

Score vs Income From FairTest (2009)

1. From the lowest scoring income group to the highest scoring income group, the approximate number of points by which the median score increases for each additional $10,000 in family income is:

The difference between the lowest income score (~455) and the highest income score (~530) is 75. The low income range differs from the high income range by $80,000. That's 75/8 = 9.375 points for every $10,000.

The answer is (C).

2! Which of the following must be true based on the Score vs. Income graph?

I.   No one whose family earns more than $80,000 scored below 500.

II.   For test-takers whose families earn between $40,000 and $60,000, there were more scores below 475 than above 475.

III. The median score of all test-takers represented in the chart is closer to 500 than it is to 525.

The *median* for rich people is ~ 530. The lowest score could be anything. So I is not true.

The median for middle income people is ~ 495 so there were the same number of scores above 495 as below 495 and II is backwards.

III is tricky. If there were a lot of people with incomes over $60k then the overall median score could be 515 or higher. The answer is (A).

3. If the rate of score increase (in points per dollar) between the lowest and second lowest income groups persisted for all income groups, at what income would the median score first reach 800?

Going from the lowest to the second lowest income group requires an extra $20k and gets you 20 points. So 17 jumps of $20,000 or $340,000 would get you the 340 points you need for an 800. The answer is (A).

Questions 4-7: Assume that people who use CrushTheTest ("users") and people who do not use CrushTheTest ("non-users") will achieve scores on the math SAT according to the table below. A test score is always a multiple of 10.

scores for 100,000 users and 1,000,000 non-users

score	users (%)	non-users (%)
800	16	1
750-790	40	10
700-740	30	20
600-690	14	30
200-590	0	39

4.   The median score for all users could be:

You know that 56% of users get 750 or above so the median must be in the 750 to 790 range. If there are an even number of scores, the median could be the average of 750 and 760 or 755.

The answer is (D).

5.   If test-takers scoring in any of the ranges in the table are equally likely to receive any score in the range, what will be the ratio of the number of non-users scoring 720 to the number of users scoring 720?

From the percentages in the table, the ratio of non-users to users would be 2 to 3 if there were the same number of each. Since there are 10 times as many non-users, the actual ratio is 20 to 3 or 6.67.

You can also calculate the number of non-users getting 720 by doing 20% divided by 5 (because there are 5 scores in the range: 700, 710, 720, 730, and 740) equals 4% and 4% of 1,000,000 is 40,000.

Next, you calculate the number of users getting 720 by doing 30% divided by 5 equals 6% and 6% of 100,000 is 6,000.

Finally, $40,000 / 6,000 = 6.67$.

Either way, the answer is (E).

Questions 4-7: Assume that people who use CrushTheTest ("users") and people who do not use CrushTheTest ("non-users") will achieve scores on the math SAT according to the table below. A test score is always a multiple of 10.

scores for 100,000 users and 1,000,000 non-users

score	users (%)	non-users (%)
800	16	1
750-790	40	10
700-740	30	20
600-690	14	30
200-590	0	39

6. If test-takers scoring in any of the ranges in the table are equally likely to receive any score in the range, how many out of a randomly-selected group of 500 non-users would be expected to receive a 650?

Since each score in a given range is equally likely, 1 out of 10 non-users scoring in the 600 to 690 range would get a 650. Since 30% are in that range, that means $30/10 = 3\%$ of all non-users get a 650. Three percent of 500 is 15 so the answer is (D).

7. If users scoring between 750 and 790 are equally likely to receive any score in that range, then, to the nearest point, the average score received by users scoring between 750 and 800 inclusive is:

There are 5 scores between 750 and 790 so each one counts for 8% ($40/5=8$). The easiest way to average the series of scores: 750 (8%), 760 (8%), 770 (8%), 780 (8%) 790 (8%) and 800 (16%) is to just count the 800 twice and do an ordinary average. The result is just under 779.

The answer is (E).

<u>Note</u>: You could also multiply each score by its percentage and then divide by the total percentage:

$$\frac{750 \cdot 8 + 760 \cdot 8 + 770 \cdot 8 + 780 \cdot 8 + 790 \cdot 8 + 800 \cdot 16}{56} = 778.57$$

Questions 8-10: The figure below shows a (fictional) STS budget.

$100,000,000 STS Budget

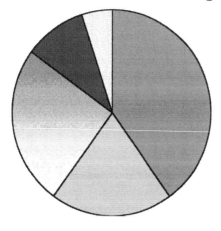

■ Salaries For Big Shots 40%

□ Public Relations 20%

▨ Salaries For Ordinary Employees 25%

■ Buildings and Supplies 10%

□ Producing Questions 5%

8. Suppose there are five times as many ordinary employees as big shots. The ratio of the average big shot salary to the average ordinary employee salary is therefore:

Suppose our fictional STS has 1 big shot who gets 40% of the budget and 5 ordinary employees who get 25% of the budget. That means each ordinary employee gets 5% of the budget compared to 40% for the big shot. That's 8 to 1 (B).

9. To produce a test question, the STS pays Joe $100 to write five proposed questions and then pays Bob $100 to pick one of the five to be an actual test question. If the average STS test has 100 questions and if questions are not re-used, how many different tests can STS inflict upon us per year?

So it costs 200 dollars to produce a question or 20,000 dollars per test. Since 5% of 100 million is 5 million, that means they can make 5 million divided by 20,000 = 250 tests. The answer is (E).

10. In response to criticism of its tests, the STS decides to increase the dollar amount of its public relations (PR) budget by 40% by allocating money from salaries for ordinary employees to PR. What is the new percentage of the budget spent on salaries for ordinary employees?

The PR budget starts out as 20% of the total. Since 40% of 20 is 8, we need to increase the PR budget from 20% of the total to 28% of the total. So 8% of the total (fictional) STS budget gets transferred to PR reducing the amount spent on ordinary employees from 25% to 17%. The answer is (A).

End of Section

Charts Tips

<u>I know! We'll just increase the PR budget.</u>

Minimizing your calculator use could be worth as much as 50 points.

If one group has a median of 10, another a median of 20, and another a median of 30, the overall median is somewhere between 10 and 30 but you can't even estimate the overall median because you don't know how many numbers are in each group.

Use an informal approach whenever possible.

Remember, the median is the physical middle and doesn't have to be one of the numbers.

A weighted average is when you count some numbers extra times because they occur more often.

As long as it's consistent with what the problem says, you are free to make up very simple numbers. This is an extremely powerful technique on a speed test composed of problems that must be solvable in two minutes.

If you get 10% of the profits, a 50% increase in the dollar amount you received means you get 15% of the profits.

A big part of the math test is careful reading.

Logic

Reasoning

multiple if-then statements, quadratics, number characteristics, long word problems, information sufficiency, define and use new symbol

Reasoning

1. Bob and Carol and Ted and Alice either hate or love each of the other three people. The following is true:

Bob loves Ted and hates Carol
Carol loves two of the other three people
Carol hates everyone who hates her
Only one person loves Alice

Therefore, which must be true:

I.   Ted hates Alice

II.   Ted loves Carol

III. Ted loves Bob

We know that Bob hates Carol and she therefore hates him back.

Since Carol hates Bob, she must love Ted and Alice.

Since only one person (Carol) loves Alice, Ted and Bob must both hate her. So I must be true.

Since Carol loves Ted, he must love her too (otherwise she would hate him) so II must be true.

We know that Bob loves Ted but we have no way of knowing if Ted loves or hates Bob so III is not necessarily true.

The answer is (D).

2. Bob and Carol and Ted and Alice smuggle treasure from a Caribbean island to the United States. The FBI is onto them. There are four possible outcomes and each of our four heroes will experience one outcome and each will experience a different outcome.

Bob or Carol or Ted will go to jail.
Ted or Alice will get rich.
Carol or Alice will change her identity.
Bob or Ted or Alice will go into hiding.

Which of the following is true?

I.   If Bob goes to jail, Alice gets rich.

II.   If Ted goes to jail, Bob goes into hiding.

III. If Carol goes to jail, Ted gets rich.

If Bob goes to jail, you could have Alice go into hiding, Carol changing her identity, and Ted getting rich. So I is NOT true.

If Ted goes to jail, Alice has to get rich. But if Ted is in jail and Alice is rich that leaves Bob to go into hiding. So II is true.

If Carol goes to jail, Alice has to change her identity. This means that Ted gets rich. So III is true.

The answer is (D).

3. If the equation below is true for all values of x and if $b>0$, then what is the value of b?

$$x^2 + 3bx + b + c = (x+b)(x+c)$$

SATAN has an unnatural fondness for "true for all values of x" problems. Essentially, these are problems with an infinite number of solutions.

For example, $x+y = x+y$ has an infinite number of solutions. You can see how dull it is. In general, if the left and right sides match up perfectly, you get infinite solutions.

In this case, after FOILing the right side we get:

$$x^2 + 3bx + b + c = x^2 + (b+c)x + bc.$$

They told us this equation is true no matter what you put in for x. The only way it will always work is if the left and right sides are *exactly* the same (*i.e.*, if they match up perfectly). Therefore,

$3b = (b+c)$ and $b+c = bc$.

The first equation gives you $2b = c$ which you can substitute into the second equation to get $3b = bc$ which gives you $3 = c$.

Plugging in this value for c, we get $2b = 3$ which gives us $b = 3/2$ and the answer (C).

Note: $b=c=0$ also works but they said $b>0$.

Try this one: $(2a+b)x+(3a+b)y = 4x+7y$ true for all x,y. What are a and b?

4. If $ax^2 + bx + c = 0$ for all values of x then which of the following is true?

I. $a = b = c = 0$

II. $a > b + c$

III. $a^2 > b^2 + c^2$

Usually, a quadratic is true for up to 2 values of x. But this one is true for ALL values of x which means it has an infinite number of solutions.

If a, b, and c were three non-zero numbers, you could solve for x by using the quadratic formula or by factoring and you would get 0, 1, or 2 answers. Even if one or two of the coefficients equals zero, you still get 0, 1, or 2 solutions.

The only way to get an infinite number of solutions is if all three coefficients are zero as in I. So the answer is (B).

5! If n is an integer, for how many values of n does $x^2 + nx + n = 0$ have integer solutions?

To get integer solutions (*e.g.*, $-a$ and $-b$), the quadratic must be factorable:

$$x^2 + nx + n = (x + a) \cdot (x + b) = x^2 + (a + b)x + ab.$$

You need pairs of integers that multiply to n AND add up to n. The product ab must equal the sum $(a+b)$. That is:

$$n = ab = a + b \implies b(a - 1) = a \implies b = \frac{a}{a - 1}.$$

That last equation on the right is very limiting. The only values of a that will give an integer for b are 2 and 0. So the only pairs (a,b) that multiply and add up to the same thing are $(2,2)$ and $(0,0)$.

So $n=4$ and $n=0$ will work and the answer is (C).

Note: Another value of a, like 3, will get you $b=3/2$ which is not an integer. Neither is $4/3$, $5/4$, or $100/99$ for that matter.

6. If $ab = cd$ and $a > b > c > d$ then which of the following must be true?

I. $a > 0$

II. $|b| = |c|$

III. $|c| < |d|$

Since a and b are both bigger than c and d but the products are the same, a and b must both be positive with c and d both negative.

Here's an example:

$$4 \cdot 3 = -2 \cdot -6.$$

So I is always true but II is not.

Since c is bigger than d but they are both negative, III must be true as it is in the example above.

The answer is (D).

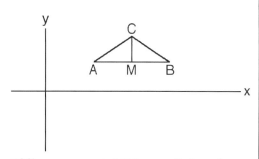

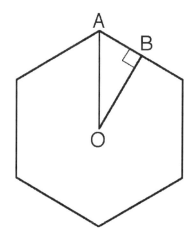

7. If line segment AB is parallel to the *x*-axis and M is the midpoint of AB and CM is perpendicular to AB, which of the following is sufficient additional information, by itself, to determine the area of triangle ABC?

    I.   the *xy* coordinates of A and C

    II.   the *xy* coordinates of A and B

    III. the *xy* coordinates of C and M

To get the area, you need the height and base.

If you're given A and C, you can subtract the *x*-coordinates and double the result to get the base. You can also subtract the *y*-coordinates to get the height. So I is enough information to get the area.

Given the coordinates of A and B, you could pick anything you like for C and get any area you want. So II isn't true.

Knowing C and M gives you the height but you could put A and B anywhere, get any base length you want, and therefore get any area you want. So III isn't true.

The answer is (B).

8. Which of the following statements would, if true, provide sufficient additional information to determine the perimeter of the regular hexagon with center O shown in the figure?

    I.   The length of AO is 2 inches.

    II.   The length of BO is 2 inches.

    III. The perimeter of ΔAOB is 2 inches.

The triangle is 30-60-90, so knowing any one side gives you all three sides.

Knowing the perimeter of ΔAOB is also enough. If *x*=AB then the perimeter (*P*) is:

$$P = x + 2x + \sqrt{3}x.$$

Given *P* you can solve for *x*. The perimeter of the hexagon is 12*x*.

So any of the three pieces of information is sufficient. The answer is (E).

9. A positive number x has three digits and $\sim x$ is defined as the number obtained by adding 1 to each digit that is less than 9 while leaving 9's unchanged. Which of the following must be true?

I. $\sim(\sim x) > \sim x$

II. $\sim x \geq x + 100$

III. $3x > \sim x$

If you hit 999 with a squiggle, nothing happens so I and II are both NOT true.

The squiggle could change 111 into 222 but doubling isn't tripling so III is true.

The answer is (D).

10. For a number n ($n \neq 0$),

$$\ddagger n = \frac{1}{n}$$

and

$$*n = 1 - \frac{1}{n}.$$

Therefore, for a number m ($m \neq 0, 1$),

$$*(\ddagger(*m)) =$$

Double dagger means "flip upside down." Starring means "flip upside down and subtract from 1."

We start on the inside and work our way out: $*m = 1 - 1/m = (m-1)/m$. The $\ddagger$ flips it to $m/(m-1)$. Finally, we star this to get:

$$1 - \frac{1}{m/(m-1)} = 1 - \frac{m-1}{m} = \frac{m}{m} - \frac{m-1}{m} = \frac{m-m+1}{m} = \frac{1}{m}$$

The answer is (B).

End of Section

Reasoning Tips

<u>You have grown powerful, my young apprentice.</u>

The answer to the "Try this one:" question in the solution to #3 is:
a=3, b=-2.

A garden variety quadratic equation has 2, 1, or zero solutions.

If a and b are limited to integers, sometimes it is possible to solve one equation with 2 unknowns.

For information sufficiency questions, ask yourself if you can make changes without contradicting the given information. If you can't make changes, enough information has been given for a solution. If you can make changes, then there must be more than one solution.

Funny symbols are intimidating (they could be anything: stars, daggers, squares, triangles etc.) but they are nothing more than "do this with the number(s)" instructions. SATAN likes funny symbols.

It's always good to make up one or two concrete examples to work with or try out. You want to be clever and tricky and keep it simple; you don't want to be Einstein.

Counting

Combinations

distribution of objects, creation of teams, combinations, combinations with exceptions, number of routes

Sequences

sum of numbers in a sequence, determination of nth number in a sequence, complex rules for determining members of a sequence

Combinations

1. Positive integer N is the product of four different prime numbers w, x, y, and z. How many different factors does N have (including itself and 1)?

You've got the prime factorization, now you just have to make all possible factors. There are 6 right off (w, x, y, z, itself, and 1). But there's also wx, wy, wz, xy, xz, and yz. But wait, there's more. There's wxy, wxz, wyz, and xyz (there are 4 ways to leave one prime factor out). You've already counted $wxyz$ because that is the number itself and since they said all the primes are different, you don't have to worry that wxy and wxz are the same thing.

Remember, primes are the atoms that make up a number. There can't be any factors of the number (except 1) that aren't made up of its primes. For example, 30 is made up of one 2, one 3, and one 5. The additional factors of 30 are 6, 10, and 15 and can all be made out of its primes.

Anyway, N has 16 different factors. The answer is (C).

2! Bob and Carol and Ted and Alice see 3 silver dollars lying on the street. They run for the money and a fight ensues. At the end of the battle, all three silver dollars are spoken for. One possible outcome is Bob has 2 of the silver dollars, Carol has 1, and Ted and Alice have none. How many such possible outcomes are there?

If you can systematically write out all the possibilities for this problem, you will be able to do it for anything you see on the real SAT.

Let's say 3000 means Bob gets 3 and everyone else gets none. That's 1.

For Bob getting 2 we have 2100 and a pair of 20's (2010 and 2001). That's 1+2.

For Bob getting 1 we have 1200, two 11's (1110 and 1101), and three 10's (1020, 1011, 1002). That's 1+2+3.

For Bob getting 0 we have 0300, two 02's (0210 and 0201), three 01's (0120, 0111, 0102), and four 00's (0030, 0021, 0012, and 0003). That's 1+2+3+4.

The total is the following cute pattern: 1 + 1+2 + 1+2+3 + 1+2+3+4 = 20.

The answer is (B).

3. One four-person team will be created from 4 boys and 4 girls. If the team must have two boys and two girls, how many different possible teams might be created?

There are equations for this sort of thing but I usually don't bother with them. First pick two boys from ABCD: AB, AC, AD, BC, BD, or CD. That's 6 possible pairs. You also get six pairs of girls: ab, ac, ad, bc, bc, or cd. Now make the team by picking one from each group. For each pair of boys you can pick any of 6 pairs of girls. So you get 6 times 6 different teams. The answer is (C).

<u>Note</u>: For a team of 2 you can also say (pick one of 4) X (pick one of 3 remaining) equals 12 and divide by 2 factorial because order doesn't matter for a simple team. You still get 6 possible teams of 2.

4. Alice, Bob, Carol, David, and Ted are going to sit down in five chairs. The chairs are numbered 1-5. Ted is superstitious and will not sit in chair #3 as he notes that SAT has three letters and has concluded, possibly erroneously, that 3 is an unlucky number. The chairs are not moved, each person chooses one chair, and Ted does not choose chair #3. In how many different ways may the five people arrange themselves among the five chairs?

When there is an "odd man" like Ted, you just do each of Ted's choices separately and then add up the results.

So Ted picks chair #1 and the others distribute themselves among chairs # 2, 3, 4, and 5 in 4 factorial = 24 ways.

If Ted picks chair #2, that's another 24 ways.

Since Ted can choose any of 4 chairs, the total number of possible arrangements is 24 times 4 equals 96 (D).

5. A group of T people were surveyed about the SAT and asked to check <u>one or two</u> of the choices below.

What is your opinion of the SAT?

    ○ it is evil

    ○ it sucks

In each of the T surveys, at least one oval was checked. A total of x "it is evil" checks were counted and a total of y "it sucks" checks were counted. The positive integer B is the number of surveys in which <u>both</u> choices were checked.

Which of the following statements must be true?

I. $x + y = T + B$

II.   The number of people who checked only "it is evil" is $x - B$.

III.   If $x = B$, everyone checked "it is evil."

Imagine two overlapping circles: one for choice 1 (x) and one for choice 2 (y). With *any* question like this, x-B pick only choice 1, y-B pick only choice 2, and $(x-B) + (y-B) + B = T - N$ is true (N people pick neither choice; $N = 0$ for this one).

So $x+y=T+B-N$ is a <u>great equation</u> for these problems and I and II are both true.

If $x = B$ then $y = T$ which means everyone checked "it sucks" (y) and the x circle is completely inside the y circle. Some people checked only "it sucks."

So III is not true and the answer is (C).

6. N points are placed on line segment AB so that, including points A and B, there are $N+2$ points on AB. The additional points are labeled A_1, A_2, A_3, *etc.*, and all possible line segments with labeled endpoints are considered (AA_1, AA_2, A_2A_3, A_2B, *etc.*). How many <u>different</u> line segments are there?

When you are making your line segment, you have $(N+2)$ choices for the first point and $(N+1)$ choices for the second point. So the total number of combinations is $(N+2)\cdot(N+1)$ BUT the line segment AA_1 and A_1A are the same line segment so you have to divide by two.

If you FOIL and divide by 2 you get the answer (E).

<u>Note</u>: If two line segments have different endpoints they are considered different line segments even if they have the same length.

7. To gain an advantage on the SAT, some students study CrushTheTest (CTT), some study previous unpublished tests obtained from friends, some study both CTT and previous tests, and some poor saps do neither. If 25% of students do neither and if the number of students who study both CTT and previous tests is half the number who study only CTT and one-third the number who study only previous tests, then what percentage of students study only CTT?

If a people do only one thing (in this case study CTT) and b people do only one other thing (in this case study previous tests) and B people do both and N people do neither then the following equation is always true:

Total People $= T = a + b + B + N$.

Since they're doing percentages we might as well assume 100 students total with $N = 25$ and then convert the words to this equation:

$$B = \frac{a}{2} = \frac{b}{3} \ .$$

Doing a little substitution (SATAN's favorite) and expressing everything in terms of B to avoid fractions we get:

$$100 = 2B + 3B + B + 25 \implies B = 12.5 \implies a = 25.$$

So the answer is (E).

Note: It's okay for B to be 12.5 because it's a percent.

8. From the secret headquarters of the fictional Standardized Testing Service (STS), three underground roads each lead directly to the big boss's office. From SATAN's office, three more roads each wind ever deeper to the Eternal Testing Center (ETC) where bad people spend all eternity taking and re-taking the SAT. How many different routes are there from STS to the ETC and back if no route can use the same road twice?

To get from STS to SATAN's office, you have 3 choices. To get from his office to the ETC you have 3 choices. To return from the ETC to SATAN's office you have 2 choices (you can't re-use a road). And to get back to STS you have 2 choices.

Now you just multiply the number of choices at each choice point.

Multiply: $3 \times 3 \times 2 \times 2 = 36$ different routes.

The answer is (D).

Note: On the other hand, one might say "none of these" because, as we know, no one returns from the ETC.

9. A teacher at the TSA (Testing School of America) finally gets fed up with giving tests. So she makes a deal with her twenty-student class: there will be no tests. At the end of the year, students will pick their grade out of a hat which will contain 20 slips of paper each with a different integer between 81 and 100 inclusive written on it. The piece of paper you pick will be your grade for the year. Pieces of paper will NOT be returned to the hat after they are picked. You have a friend in the class whose name is Joe. What is the probability that you and Joe will be within one point of each other after you have each picked a grade?

How many *different* pairs can you make from 20 objects? The short answer is 20 times 19 divided by 2 or 190. Since 19 of those pairs are within one point of each other, the answer is $19/190 = 1/10$ or (A).

Note 1: The "different pairs" formula comes from 20 choices for the first number times 19 choices for the second number divided by 2 so you don't count both (81, 82) and (82, 81).

Note 2: Your chances of picking 82 through 99 are 18/20 in which case Joe has a 2/19 chance of getting within 1 point of your grade. Your chances of picking 81 or 100 is 2/20 in which case Joe has a 1/19 chance of being within 1 point of your grade. Overall:

$$\frac{18}{20} \cdot \frac{2}{19} + \frac{2}{20} \cdot \frac{1}{19} = \frac{18}{190} + \frac{1}{190} = \frac{19}{190} = \frac{1}{10}$$

10. If a, b, and c are positive integers, how many ordered triplets (a, b, c) satisfy the equation below?

$$a^3 \cdot b^2 \cdot c = 64$$

You have to do it systematically or you'll miss one.

First make a as big as it can be. You get (4, 1, 1).

There's no other way to have $a = 4$ so now you can move on to $a = 2$. If a is 2, the biggest b can be is 2 and this gives (2, 2, 2). It is also possible for b to be 1 which gives (2, 1, 8).

It's important to start with the biggest possible b and work your way down. That's the idea of "being systematic."

Now we can move on to $a = 1$. The biggest b can be now is 8 which gives (1, 8, 1). You can also have (1, 4, 4) and (1, 2, 16) and (1, 1, 64).

That's a total of 7 possibilities. The answer is (E).

End of Section

Combinations Tips

Soon you will be one of us.

The number of pairs possible with N objects is N times N-1 because you have N choices for the first and N-1 choices for the second.

BUT if order does not matter, you have to divide by 2. The team of Bob and Joe is the same as the team of Joe and Bob so if you are doing teams of two with six people there are 6·5/2 = 15 possible teams.

On the other hand, if you are doing president/vp pairs with six people (think McCain/Palin vs Palin/McCain) then the answer is 30 pairs.

N objects can be arranged in N! different ways because you have N choices for the first object times N-1 choices for the second object times N-2 choices for the third object etc.

If you have 3 groups (say pants, shirts, and shoes) with N, M, and P objects in each one then you have N choices times M choices times P choices when you are picking your outfit.

If you have 4 things, say the numbers 1, 2, 3, and 4, and you are going to make a 3-digit number and 111 is allowed then you have 4 choices times 4 choices times 4 choices.

Note how you are always just multiplying the choices so you don't really have to remember any formulas.

If there's no obvious way to calculate the number of possibilities you just have to write them out and you have to be systematic about it.

If there are T people and x do one thing and y do another thing and B do both and N do neither then $T = x + y - B + N$.

If there are T people and a do ONLY one thing and b do ONLY another thing and B do both and N do neither then $T = a + b + B + N$..

Sequences

1. What is the last digit in 7^{503} ?

$7^1 = 7; 7^2 = 49; 7^3 = ...3; 7^4 = ...1; 7^5 = ...7$.

The trick is to worry ONLY about the last digit. The last digit of 7 cubed has to be 3 because when you multiply 49 by 7, the first thing you get is 63. Multiplying by 7 again the first thing you get is 7 times 3 = 21 so the last digit in 7^4 has to be 1.

The pattern goes 7, 9, 3, 1, 7, 9, 3, 1, 7 . . .

The group of four {7, 9, 3, 1} repeats. The last digit of 7^{500} is a 1 because $500/4 = 125$ and we have exactly 125 groups. At 7^{501} we start over again at 7. So the last digit in 7^{503} is 3.

The answer is (B).

2. The fraction 1/7 is equal to 0.142857142857 . . . The first digit after the decimal point is 1. What is the sum of the first 100 digits after the decimal point?

Each group of 6 has a sum of 1+4+2+8+5+7=27. There are 16 such groups in 100 and 16 times 27 is 432. But 16 groups of 6 is only 96 digits. You need to add on a 1, a 4, a 2, and an 8:

$27 \cdot 16 + 1 + 4 + 2 + 8 = 447$.

The answer is (E).

3. In the sequence 1, 2, 3, 1, 2, 3 . . . the first digit is a 1, the second digit is a 2, the third digit is a 3, the fourth digit is a 1 *etc.* A subset S of this sequence consists of every 10th digit starting with the 10th digit, the 20th digit, and the 30th digit, up to and including the 1000th digit. There are 100 digits in subset S. What is the sum of the digits in subset S?

The 10th digit is a 1, the 20th is a 2, the 30th is a 3, the 40th is a 1 again. So you are really just adding up the first 100 digits of the sequence 1, 2, 3, 1, 2, 3, . . .

For this sequence, we have repeating groups of 3 and the sum of each group is 1+2+3=6.

There are 33 groups of 3 in the first 100 digits so that's 33 times 6 = 198 for the sum of the first 99 digits.

The 100th digit is a 1 so the final sum is 199.

The answer is (C).

$$x, \ldots, a$$

4. In the sequence shown above, the first term is x and the 6th term is a. If each term in the sequence after the first is obtained by dividing the previous term by 2 and then squaring the result, which of the expressions below gives the value of x in terms of the value of a?

Here are all the terms:

2nd term $= \left(\dfrac{x}{2}\right)^2 = \dfrac{x^2}{4}$,

3rd term $= \left(\dfrac{x^2/4}{2}\right)^2 = \left(\dfrac{x^2}{8}\right)^2 = \dfrac{x^4}{2^6}$,

4th term $= \left(\dfrac{x^4/2^6}{2}\right)^2 = \left(\dfrac{x^4}{2^7}\right)^2 = \dfrac{x^8}{2^{14}}$,

5th term $= \left(\dfrac{x^8/2^{14}}{2}\right)^2 = \left(\dfrac{x^8}{2^{15}}\right)^2 = \dfrac{x^{16}}{2^{30}}$,

6th term $= \left(\dfrac{x^{16}/2^{30}}{2}\right)^2 = \left(\dfrac{x^{16}}{2^{31}}\right)^2 = \dfrac{x^{32}}{2^{62}}$.

We have to set the 6th term equal to a and solve for x. We multiply both sides by 2^{62} and then take both sides so the power of $(1/32)$. Here it is:

$$a = \dfrac{x^{32}}{2^{62}} \implies x^{32} = 2^{62} \cdot a \implies x = 2^{\frac{62}{32}} \cdot a^{\frac{1}{32}}.$$

This doesn't seem to match any of the choices BUT 62/32 reduces to 31/16 so the answer is (B).

$a, \ldots$

5. In the sequence above, the terms are numbered by the positive integer n. The first term in the sequence ($n = 1$) is a. Terms of the sequence after the first that have odd values of n are obtained by dividing the previous term by 2. Terms of the sequence that have even values of n are obtained by multiplying the previous term by 10. What is the 89th term in the sequence?

Always write out a few terms so you can see the pattern:

a, $10a$, $5a$, $50a$, $25a$, $250a$, $125a$, . . .

So the odd-numbered terms are are just a times some power of 5 which eliminates all answers except A and B.

Here are three odd-numbered terms:

3rd term $= 5a$

5th term $= 5^2 a$

7th term $= 5^3 a$.

The power of 5 is related to the number of the term, n, like so: power $= (n\text{-}1)/2$.

So the power is 44 and the answer is (A).

$a, b, \ldots$

6. In the sequence above, the first term is positive integer a and the second term is positive integer b. Each term after the second term is equal to the sum of the two immediately preceding terms. The ratio of the 8th term in the sequence to the third term in the sequence is 11. Which of the following could be the value of the product ab?

Here are the terms:

3rd term $= a + b$

4th term $= a + 2b$

5th term $= 2a + 3b$

6th term $= 3a + 5b$

7th term $= 5a + 8b$

8th term $= 8a + 13b$

Therefore,

$$\frac{8a + 13b}{a + b} = 11 \implies 8a + 13b = 11a + 11b \implies \frac{b}{a} = \frac{3}{2}$$

So we need two positive integers whose ratio is 3 to 2 and whose product is one of the choices. The pairs (a,b) that have the right ratio are $(2,3)$ or $(4,6)$ or $(6,9)$ *etc.* The first one that matches is the answer. In this case, it's $6 \cdot 9 = 54$.

The answer is (E).

7. A sequence of integers is numbered from 1 to n where n is the position of the integer in the sequence. The nth term of the sequence ($n>1$) is obtained by multiplying the value of the previous term by -1 and then taking the result to the power of -n. Thus, if the first term is a, the second term is $(-a)^{-2}$. If the second term is b, the third term is $(-b)^{-3}$. If the value of the first term in the sequence is 1, what is the value of the sum of the first ten terms in the sequence?

Remember, a negative power just means "make a fraction."

Here are the first five terms in the sequence:

First term: +1
Second term: $(-1)^{-2} = +1$
Third term: $(-1)^{-3} = -1$
Fourth term: $(--1)^{-4} = +1$
Fifth term: $(-1)^{-5} = -1$.

The first two terms are +1 and the next 8 terms alternate between –1 and +1.

The 3rd to 10th terms all cancel in pairs and you are left with $1 + 1 = 2$, perhaps the first bit of math you ever learned (who knew the SAT was so easy?).

The answer is (D).

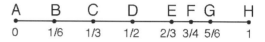

A   B   C   D   E   F   G   H
0   1/6   1/3   1/2   2/3 3/4 5/6   1

8. On the number line shown above, the length of line segment AH is 1 and the distances of points B, C, D, E, F, and G from point A have the fractional values shown. If all possible pairs of different labeled points are considered and if the length of each line segment, including AH, is calculated, how many different lengths will be obtained?

The quick way is to do everything in 12ths. So instead of using:

$$0, \ \frac{1}{6}, \ \frac{1}{3}, \ \frac{1}{2}, \ \frac{2}{3}, \ \frac{3}{4}, \ \frac{5}{6}, \ 1$$

use:

$$\frac{0}{12}, \ \frac{2}{12}, \ \frac{4}{12}, \ \frac{6}{12}, \ \frac{8}{12}, \ \frac{9}{12}, \ \frac{10}{12}, \ \frac{12}{12}.$$

The possible distances from point to point (aka the lengths of the line segments) are obtained from the possible differences of those numbers.

Since the points have to be different, you can't get a length of zero. However you can get every other length between 1/12 and 12/12 inclusive except for 11/12.

So the answer is 11 or (E).

9. Four consecutive, positive, even integers a, b, c, and d will be chosen such that $0<a<b<c<d$. If the sum, S, of the four integers must be less than 500, which of the following is the number of possible values of S?

The first possible set of consecutive, positive, even integers a, b, c, d is 2, 4, 6, and 8. You need to find the last possible set and then figure out how many sets there are.

Obviously the last set is with numbers around $500/4 = 125$. In particular, it is 120, 122, 124, 126.

Note that $122 + 124 + 126 + 128 = 500$ and so is excluded because the sum must be less than 500.

So the first set starts with 2 and the last set starts with 120 and you count by 2's. The even numbers 2, 4, 6, 8 . . . 120 have 60 members so there are 60 sets a, b, c, d and the answer is (B).

$$a, b, c, a, a, b, b, c, c, a, a, a, \ldots$$

10. In a sequence containing the letters a, b, and c, shown above, the number of repetitions of a given letter increases by 1 each time the letter reappears. In the first 90 terms of this sequence, how many times does the letter b appear?

First, ask an easier question. How many b's are there after 5 sets of abc? That's easy enough, there's $1+2+3+4+5 =15$ b's and a total of 45 letters.

The total number of letters in n sets is:

Total Letters $= 3 \cdot (1 +2+3+4+5+6+ \ldots +n)$.

If you add up 7 sets, you get 28 of each letter and $3 \cdot 28 = 84$ letters total. The next letters will be 8 a's which will take you past 90.

So there are 28 b's in the first 90 terms of the sequence (and 28 c's and 34 a's).

The answer is (A).

End of Section

Sequences Tips

Your journey is complete.

A sequence like 2, 5, 3, 9, 2, 5, 3, 9. . . consists of groups of 4 numbers. The group size is crucial. The 40,002nd term is 5 because there are 10,000 complete groups of 4 and then two more.

With "last digit," "units digit," and "ones digit" problems, you often just pay attention to the last digit and ignore the others.

Sometimes you have to write out the first few terms and look for the pattern.

Sometimes the numbers get too big and you must use exponents.

You can get rid of an exponent (like 11/20) by taking both sides to the reciprocal power (20/11).

Writing the first term or terms and the last term or terms with dots in between can be useful.

Sometimes you have to get every term.

You may have the right answer but it may not look exactly like their answer.

If you have a nasty sequence and a nasty question try asking yourself a simpler question about it to get started.

$$1+2+3+4+5+6 + . . . + n = n \cdot (n+1)/2.$$

Problems restricted to positive integers often require trial and error and you may have 1 equation and 2 unknowns.

GOOD LUCK ON THE REAL THING! — CTT

Answers

DON'T LOOK!

The answers are on the back of this page. Cut them out and give them to your assistant. Tell your assistant not to tell you the answers no matter what. They are only allowed to tell you whether or not you got 10 out of 10 on a section.

Only this and nothing more.

See page 2 for details about the CrushTheTest 10-out-of-10-or-nothing Training Technique.

DON'T COMPROMISE!

Answers

Algebra: Warmup	CBDCDDEEAE
Algebra: Manipulation	CACEECDADC
Algebra: Fractions	BAEBEDBCCB
Algebra: Functions	ACAABEAEDB
Algebra: Word Problems	DEAECCBEAB
Geometry: Lengths, Angles, . . .	BDABCEDADE
Geometry: Areas	AECDDBBDBE
Geometry: Triangles	BEDEAEEDAD
Geometry: Points and Space	CBCCEEDDCA
Units: Prices, Percents, 2D, 3D	BECDDACCAE
Units: Algebra	ACCBACBABB
Statistics: Warmup	CBBEABEDCE
Statistics: Averages	AADDDEBBDB
Statistics: Probability	ABADBDDEBD
Statistics: Mean, Median, Mode	ACCEAADABA
Numbers: Divisibility	BEEBABCDDC
Numbers: Characteristics	DCDDACAADB
Numbers: Remainders	DCCAEDACDA
Numbers: Digitology	ADBCBEDEBE
Reading: Charts	CAADEDEBEA
Logic: Reasoning	DDCBCDBEDB
Counting: Combinations	CBCDCEEDAE
Counting: Sequences	BECBAEDEBA

Questions Index

Done them all?

Want to do it again without answer choices?

Step up to the plate!
(Some questions have been altered to fit the space.)

Section	Q. #	Those sweet, sweet memories!
Manipulation	1	Charge y dollars per day, get 20 tip, divide amongst five people, spend 6 dollars, now have z dollars. How many days?
	2	If $9^{(b+1)} = a^8$ then what is 27^b in terms of a?
	3	If $x = 2b$, $a = 3$ then what is $2^{(a-b)}/2^x$ in terms of b?
	4	If $r+s+t = r-u = s-t$ then $r=-2t$? $s+t+u=0$? $r+2s=2(s-t)$?
	5	If $x = (ab+c)/a$ then what is xb in terms of x, a, and c?
	6	If $x^{8/3} = y^{6/7}$ then what is $x^2 \cdot y^{-3/7}$ in terms of x?
	7!	If $a^2 = b^2 = c^2 = d^2$ then the avg. of a, b, c, d in terms of a could be?
	8	If $2^{|-x-y|} = 1/2^{-x-y}$ then $x>-y$? $x<-y$? $x>y$? $x<y$?
	9	If $y + 2^{x+2} = 2^{x+3}$ then what is $2^{(x+2)/2}$ in terms of y?
	10	If $(x+y)/(x-y) = a$ then what is y in terms of a and x?

Section	Q. #	Don't let SATAN win!
Fractions	1	Half of a small bucket is $3/10$ of a big bucket. What is b/s?
	2	Find fraction of s to fill $1/3$ of big bucket given $s = 0.8b$.
	3	If $(1/4)x + 2x = 10$, what is $(3/4)x + 2x + x$?
	4	If $px + py = x/2 = y/3$, what is p?
	5	What is $1/3$ of $1/5$ of (1 minus $1/3$ of $1/2$)?
	6	Divide \$100 among 4 people. What whole number ratios work?
	7!	If $(1/4)x + y = 10$ and $(3/4)x + y + x = 20$, what is y/x?
	8	5-year STS exec. gets 2 hr. lunch, Joe gets 3 hrs. 40 min lunch, lunch time is directly proportional to seniority. What is Joe's seniority?
	9	If $a^2 - a^2b^2 + b^2 = 0$, what is $1/(1/a^2 + 1/b^2)$?
	10	$y = (1-x^2)/(1-1/x^2)$. $\sqrt{y} > 0$? $|y| = -y$? $y/x < 0$? $x^2 + y^2 > 1$?
Functions	1	What is the relationship between $2 \cdot f(x+90) + 2$ and $f(x)$?
	2	How do you recognize the graph of $x^3 + 5x^2 + 6x$?
	3	If $y = f(x) > 0$ and (a, b) is between $f(x)$ and the x-axis, is $f(a) > b$?
	4	Origin to $(x, \sqrt{x}) = \sqrt{6}$ (hypotenuse). x-axis is leg. Area of right Δ?
	5	$f(x) = x^2 + x + 2$. Rewrite $f(x+2)$ as a polynomial.
	6	$f(x) = 4x^2 + 6$. If $f(x)/2 = f(2x)$. What is x?
	7	Find all possible positive slopes of lines intersecting $y = x^2 - 2$ at (a, b) and $(3, c)$ with $a < 0$.
	8	Parabolas intersect vertices of rectangle with width 4 at $(2, px^2)$ and $(2, qx^2)$. What is area of rectangle in terms of p and q?
	9!	Equilateral triangle intersects $y = 2x^2$ at $(a/2, a^2/2)$. If one corner is at origin, what is area of triangle?
	10	Distance vs time graph: what does a sudden stop look like?

Section	Q. #	As God is my witness, they'll never trick me again!
Word Problems	1	$54 = x{-}10{+}(10{+}7{+}7{+}x)/3$. Find x.
	2	Triangle, area 10, height increases by 2, find change in area.
	3	20% faster motorcycle. Slow: $d = r(120)$; Fast: $d = 1.2rt$. $t=?$
	4	Joe escapes from STS thugs. Joe: $50=rt$; Thugs: $60=150t$. $r=?$
	5	If reduce width, length 20% each, area down by 12. Original area?
	6	2 squares, A and B. $a^2 = b^2{+}30$; $4a = 4b{+}8$. Solve for a.
	7	Multiply one number by 18, average doubles. Ratio of numbers?
	8	Granny car: $d = r{\cdot}8$; your car: $d=(r{+}35){\cdot}6$. $r+35=?$
	9	Alice makes as much in a month as Bill in half a year. Total income is 168000. What does Alice make per month?
	10	Big is one more than square root of Small. Big+Small could be?
Lengths . . .	1	Right triangle in circle, hypotenuse is diameter, area of circle is 20π. Get sum of squares of legs.
	2	Isosceles triangle in isosceles triangle. Areas are 5:1. Heights equal. Get ratios of all base segments.
	3!	Line tangent to $x^2 + y^2 = 10$ at (a, b). Get y-intercept in terms of b.
	4	Octagon ABCDEFG. Get AD in terms of side length.
	5	Perpendicular chord divides diameter into 2 and 8. Chord length?
	6	Circle with $r=10$ tangent to midpoint of top of 14x14 square. Bottom corner of square through circle center to circle edge has length?
	7	5 sided figure. 100°, 110° angles, 2 angles add to 180°. Get last angle.
	8	30-60-90 Δ in 30-70-80 Δ. One missing angle is x. Find all angles.
	9!	Pyramid of N 125 cc cubes has outside edge 300 cm. $N = ?$
	10!	If $7+y$ is one more than $5+x$ what is y in terms of x?

Section	Q. #	SATAN has pointy teeth.
Areas	1	Area of equilateral triangle in circle with radius 2.
	2	Fraction of square occupied by 4 tangent circles (radius = side/4).
	3	Area of square in circle with an area of 6.
	4	Area of circle around square around circle with area 1.
	5	3 equal touching circles (r=1). Get funny-shaped area in between.
	6	Rectangle and rt. Δ have same area, same height. Ratio of bases?
	7	Half of the region of a square not occupied by an inscribed circle has an area equal to 1. What is the radius of the circle?
	8	Square corner at center of circle. Sector is what fraction of square?
	9	Sector arc=1. Double angle, double area of circle. New sector arc?
	10!	Double vertex angle of isosceles Δ. What happens to area?
Triangles	1	Find largest possible right triangle with hypotenuse of 6.
	2	Base of triangle equals height. Rt. Δ? Angle opposite base = 90°? Angle opposite base <45°?
	3	Oblique Δ XYZ, height h, base XY. h>XY? h<XY? h>XZ? h<XZ?
	4	n integer, Δ lengths n+10, n+12. Shortest 3rd side if an integer?
	5	Given line through (0,0), (4,3), find x-intercept of ⊥ through (4,3).
	6	How many equilateral Δ's can be inscribed in an equilateral Δ?
	7	Equilateral Δ ABC: C (0,0), B (1,0), A (1/2, √3/2). Find length of shortest line from (1/4, 0) to AC.
	8	Δ ABC 1x1x1 with 45-45-90 BDE inside. E on BC. Find DE.
	9	Δ ABC 1x1x1, with equilateral DEF inside. DE ⊥ BC. Find DE.
	10!	Δ ABC 1x1x1 with isosceles MPQ inside. M midpt. of BC. MP ⊥ AC and MQ ⊥ AB. MP = MQ. Find PQ.

Section	Q. #	How many SAT proctors to screw in a lightbulb?
Points & Space	1	Length of body diagonal of 3 by 4 by 5 rectangular prism.
	2	Area of Δ with sides x-axis, $y=x$, $y=-(1/2)x +3$?
	3!	Rectangle has perimeter of 20 . What are possible areas?
	4	AB = 5, AC = 6, BC = 3. How many possible C's in plane?
	5	AB = 5, BC = 4, AC>4. How many possible C's in a plane?
	6	AB = 6 with midpoint M, MC = 4, BD = 2. CD = x. Find all x's.
	7	AB = 24, AC=BC=15, AD=BD=13. CD = x. Find all x's.
	8	Bisect the angle that bisects the angle that bisects the angle. Find number of different angle measures.
	9	Card with pink, red, blue, gray quadrants I - IV rotates $90n$ (n integer) degrees in 2D space. Draw all possible resulting cards.
	10	Opaque cube with ABCDEF on sides glued to ABCGHI cube and placed on opaque table. Minimum number of visible letters?
Prices . . .	1	Start with 1000, get 50% increase 4 years in a row. Now have?
	2	Equation if x percent interest over 10 years causes 12-fold increase.
	3	Lose 1/3 each time. Try 5 times. End with 32. Start with how much?
	4	What percent markup followed by 20% off gives original price?
	5	Sell x percent of 1/3, y percent of rest. Find percent of whole sold.
	6	Convert 72 km/hr to revs/min if radius is 30 cm.
	7	Small cube with 24 cm² surface area. Large 8 cm cube. Volume ratio?
	8!	Cube. Surface area a, edges $p/12$. Why can't $a = p^2$?
	9	If 1 liter of paint covers 100 square feet, how thick is the paint.
	10	Lateral area of cylinder is numerically equal to volume. Volume is?

Section	Q. #	What is the average misery level at the TSA?
Units Algebra	1	G gallons fills 6 tubs, how many tubs will $N/5$ gallons fill?
	2	If n cockroaches cost d dollars, how much for n^3 cockroaches?
	3	Drive each third at 30, 20, and 15 mph. What is average speed?
	4	n lubers do x cars a year each and y cars get 3 lubes each, what is n?
	5	d degrees for x not correct, N people get p percent of Q questions right. How much hotter does Hell get (in terms of d, x, N, p, Q)?
	6	n pianos tuned once a year by t tuners for $\$d/5$. Get tuner income.
	7	Radius r wheels to go 5 times around radius R track. Rotations?
	8	x morons, N people, 30% of nonmorons are stupid. Percent stupid?
	9	72 stupids and morons, 20 go down, horizontal morons/horizontal stupids = 4, 10 percent of stupids unconscious. Morons on the floor?
	10	N people, one third teetotalers, y ounces per bottle, 3 hour party, drinkers drink 6 oz/hr. Number of bottles consumed?
Averages	1	Take 5 tests. Score x, x–4, x–8, x–12, x–16. What is overall average?
	2	N–1 tests. Average A. Zero on Nth test. Average drops how much?
	3	If the average of 4 positive numbers is 70, can one number be 300?
	4	Five pos. integers avg. to 50, one is 26. Largest could be how big?
	5	Four numbers, average is y, one is y–12. What is average of other 3?
	6	Grp. 1 (n=120) avg. 62. Grp. 2 avg. 70. Overall avg. 67. Grp. 2 n=?
	7	$\$30$/hr get d dollars; $\$45$/hr get d dollars. Average dollars/hour?
	8	Avg. of a and b is x. Avg. a, b, c, d is 1.5b. a/b=3. Avg. of c, d is?
	9	Avg. integers, $a<b<c<d = x$. Avg. a^2, b^2, c^2, $d^2 = y$. $y>2$? $y=x^2$? $y>x$?
	10!	Average of 5 different integers is 20. Largest is 23. Smallest is N. How many possible values of N are there?

A166

Section	Q. #	Just how mean can mean get?
Probability	1	Marbles. green=(3·yellow); blue=(4·green). Prob. of picking yellow?
	2	N marbles, m colors. Pick how many to guarantee 2 of same color?
	3	P_blue=1/2; P_green=1/3; yellow=20. Find blue, green, P_yellow.
	4	green = 2·yellow = x; P_blue = 4/5. Number of blue in terms of x?
	5	yellow:green:blue=4:1:1. solid:hollow=5:1. P_(solid, green) = ?
	6	P_explode=1/9. If explode then blue. blue=162=2/3 total. What is ratio of exploding blue to all blue?
	7	P_yellow = $1/n$. What is (yellow)/(not yellow)?
	8	Write 1 to 100 in a line of digits. P_(digit is a 1)?
	9	240 say NO; 100 say MAYBE; 20 say YES. Ask 90, how many NO?
	10	What is 30% of 80% plus 10% of 20%?
MMM	1	a, b, c, d with mean x, median y. $x \neq y$? $y \neq a$? $x < 4y$?
	2!	$0 < a < b < c < d$, mean x, median y. $x < y/2$? $y = b$? $x > c$?
	3	Odd number of integers, mean x, median y, mode z. x integer? y integer? z integer?
	4	Integers a, b, c, $a > b > c$, $a = 12$, $c = 2$. Median = mean+2. Find median.
	5	$a < b < c < d$, median = mean. $b - a = d - c$? $c + d = 2(a+b)$? $d = 4a$? $a + c = b + d$?
	6	N consecutive integers, mean A, median M. $M - A =$?
	7	1, 2, 4, 8, 16, 32 . . .mean>median? median integer? mean integer?
	8	5 consecutive positive integers. Double smallest. What happens to mean and median?
	9	x, $4x$, $5x$, $5x$-2. Only one equal pair. Could mode be x? $4x$? $5x$?
	10	Given nine positive numbers. You can change two. You must decrease the median and increase the mean. Watcha gonna do?

Section	Q. #	We hope you get into Caltech.
Divisibility	1	If n is a factor of x then is $x+15n$ divisible by n? 5? x?
	2	$x=pqr$; p, q, r prime; $r>q>p$. Prime factor of x bigger than r? Prime factor less than p? x^2 divisible by p, q, and r?
	3!	$2jk+1$ divisible by k? divisible by 3? not prime? must be prime?
	4!	$k^2n+p^2=Qkn$, integers>1, p prime. $Q=p$? $k=n$? $kn<p^2$? $kn>p^2$? $Q=p+2$?
	5	$n\cdot(k-6n)=11$; k, n are integers>1. Find k.
	6	$j>k>0$; j, k divisible by 2, 3, 5. Minimum value of $j-k$?
	7	$j>k>0$; j, k divisible by 2, 3, 8. Minimum value of $j-k$?
	8	12^{100} divisible by 18? 24? 27? 30? 36?
	9	$N=pqr$; $p>q>r$ (p, q, r prime). Is p greater than cube root of N? Is N/p^2 an integer? Is N^2/p an integer?
	10	$p^2-n^2=3Q$; Q prime>3; p, n integers>0. Find Q in terms of n.
Characteristics	1	If $x^3<x<x^2$ then what is true about x?
	2	If $x<x^3<x^2$ then what is true about x?
	3!	If $x>y$ and $x\neq0$ and $y\neq0$ then $x^2>y^2$? $1/x>1/y$? $1/x<1/y$? $x^3>y^3$?
	4!	Given $x+2y>2x-3y$. $x/y<5$? x could be $>y$? if $y<0$, then $x<0$?
	5	If $r<s<t$ then $rs<st$? $|1/r|>|1/s|$? $s^2>r$?
	6	How do you make $1/|2-x|$ increase?
	7	If a is an integer and $b=a^3$ then what could $\sqrt{b}$ be?
	8	Even or odd? Odd to odd power, odd to even power, even to odd power, sum of odds, even times odd.
	9	j,k integers; $2j+4=k$ then j even? k even? jk even?
	10	$xw+yz+yw+xz$ is odd. If x odd then y even? $xyzw$ odd? $x+w$ even?

Section	Q. #	Beware the odd remainder.
Remainders	1!	n, k integers>1. Remainder of $(4kn+6k+2)/6k$ could be 1? $4k$? $2k+2$?
	2	$N/70$ has remainder 58. Today is Monday, what day in N days?
	3	$n/90$ has remainder 1. Remainder of $(n+179)/90$ and $(n+182)/90$?
	4	Divide n, $n+7$, $n+18$, $n+21$, $n+29$, $n+32$ by 11. How many remainders?
	5	What are possible remainders when n and $2n$ are divided by 5?
	6	If divisor is, say, 10, what are the possible remainders?
	7	If $j<k$ and $j/k = x$ with remainder y, find x and y.
	8	If $k<j<2k$ and $j/k = x$ with remainder y, find x and y.
	9	$N/23$ has remainder 11. What is remainder of $4N/23$?
	10	$N<100$. $N/6$ has remainder 5. $N/3$ has remainder 1. How many N's?
Digitology	1	AA + BB = BBC. Find A, B, and C.
	2	AB+B=BA. Find A and B.
	3!	Add 185 consecutive integers. Find all possible units digits of sum.
	4	a,b integers>0. ab has units digit 2. a-b could have what units digits?
	5!	AB+CD divisible by 10. If A+B=8 is D-A=2? How many values of AB? Smallest possible CD?
	6	4 digit x (ABCD), A+B+C+D=N. Sum of digits of $2x$ could be N? N-12? N+10?
	7	$1/x = 0.0B$. $1/y = 0.00A$. Bx/Ay=?
	8	Q, R integers. $1/Q = 0.0A$, $1/R=0.0B$. Product of A and B could be?
	9	If order matters, how many different sequences of 3 letters are there?
	10	3 wheels with 0, 1, 2, 3. Right wheel rotates 90° per sec. Middle wheel rotates 90° every 4 sec. Left wheel 90° every 16 sec. Reading at 60 sec?

A169

Section	Q. #	How much does an 800 cost?
Charts	1	450 to 540 costs $90k. How many points do you get for $10k?
	2!	Medians of 5 groups are 450, 470, 500, 520 and 540. Overall median?
	3	If 450 to 480 requires $20k. How much to get an 800?
	4	If all scores are divisible by 10 is median always divisible by 10?
	5	What is ratio of 20% of 1,000,000 to 30% of 100,000?
	6	If 30 percent get 600-690, what percent get 650 (if even distr.)?
	7	40% 750-790; 16% 800. What is average of all scores 750-800?
	8	5 pawns get 25%; 1 hot shot gets 40%. What is hot shot/pawn?
	9	$200/question; 100 questions/test; $20 million. How many tests?
	10	Start with 20% of total, increase this by 40%, what is new % of total?
Reasoning	1	If Carol always returns hate with hate, and she loves you, does that mean you love her?
	2	If Carol can either go to jail or change her identity and Bob goes to jail, what happens to Carol?
	3	If $ax^2+bx+c = dx^2+ex+f$ for all x, what is true about a, b, c, d, e, f?
	4	If $ax^2+bx+c = 0$ for all x, what is true about a, b, c?
	5!	a, b, n integers, $x^2+nx+n=(x+a)(x+b)$ is true for how many n's?
	6	$a>b>c>d$, $ab=cd$. $a>0$? $|b|=|c|$? $|c|<|d|$?
	7	$\triangle ABC$ (isosceles, $AC=BC$) with M midpoint of AB. The coordinates of which points are necessary to determine the area?
	8	Given a 30-60-90 $\triangle$, can you get all three sides from the perimeter?
	9	~ means add one to each digit except 9. What is the most ~ can do to a 3-digit number?
	10	1 minus the inverse of the inverse of 1 minus the inverse of x is?

Section	Q. #	It is best to avoid the Eternal Testing Center.
Combinations	1	$N=wxyz$ (w, x, y, z prime). How many factors does N have?
	2!	How many ways can you distribute 3 dollars among 4 people?
	3	Want a 4 person team (2 boys, 2 girls). Have 4 boys, 4 girls. How many possible teams?
	4	Five people, five chairs. Ted avoids chair #3. How many ways to sit?
	5	x do X, y do Y, B do both, T total people, N do none. Find equation relating x, y, B, T, and N.
	6	Line segment with $N+2$ labeled points. # of different segments?
	7	a do only A, b do only B, B do both, T total, N neither. Find equation relating a, b, B, T, and N.
	8	3 roads A to B, 3 B to C. A to C and back with no repeat roads?
	9	20 #'s 81 to 100. Bob, Joe pick 1 each. Prob. Bob and Joe within 1?
	10	a, b, c integers>0, $a^3b^2c=64$. Number of (a, b, c)'s?
Sequences	1	Last digit in 7^{503}?
	2	What is the sum of the first 100 digits in the decimal of $1/7$?
	3	1, 2, 3, 1, 2, 3, . . . Sum of every 10th digit up to 1000th digit?
	4	x, $(x/2)^2$, . . . a. If a is 6th term, find x in terms of a.
	5	a, $10a$, $5a$, $50a$, $25a$, . . . Find 89th term.
	6	a, b, $a+b$, $a+2b$, $2a+3b$, . . . Ratio of 8th term to 3rd term is 11. If a and b are positive integers then ab could be?
	7	a, $(-a)^{-2}$, . . . b, $(-b)^{-n}$. If $a=1$, what is the sum of the first 10 terms?
	8	Number line, 8 labeled points: 0, $1/6$, $1/3$, $1/2$, $2/3$, $3/4$, $5/6$, 1. How many different lengths between labeled points?
	9	Consecutive even integers $0<a<b<c<d$. Sum < 500. # of diff. sums?
	10	a, b, c, a, a, b, b, c, c, a, a, a, . . . How many b's in first 90 terms?

About the Author

Matthew Kohler received his Ph.D. in physics from the University of Colorado at Boulder in 1992. His dissertation research was conducted at the Tri-University Meson Facility (TRIUMF) in Vancouver, British Columbia. He crashed subatomic particles called pions into other subatomic particles called deuterons and counted how many pions bounced in which direction. Of course, Matt's papers published in *Physical Review* did not include the word "bounce."

Matt had learned previously that bouncing pions are viewed suspiciously by some. When an exhausted, unshaven graduate student trying to get back into the U.S. answered the "what were you doing in Canada?" question with the brief, but accurate, "bouncing pions," he was asked to pull over and await interrogation. He was not arrested but he almost missed his plane.

Dr. Kohler taught physics for several years at Bridgewater State College in Massachusetts and then moved back to Colorado to found CrushTheTest. At his Boulder office, Matt provides tutoring in algebra, geometry, trigonometry, precalculus, calculus, statistics, chemistry, and physics as well as SAT and ACT prep.

In 2006, Dr. Kohler published "Finding the Missing Time in the Instantaneous Turnaround Version of the Twin Paradox" in *Foundations of Physics Letters*. Before *Foundations* published Dr. Kohler's paper, imaginary astronauts were routinely and unceremoniously squashed when their spaceships traveling at nearly the speed of light instantly reversed direction to go back to Earth. Dr. Kohler showed that all this carnage is unnecessary; the ship can reverse direction gradually and the math involved won't strangle your friendly neighborhood physics major.

The fine work you are perusing at the moment is Dr. Kohler's first book.